THE
TREASURE
INSIDE
YOUR
CHILD

PAM FARREL

HARVEST HOUSE PUBLISHERS
Eugene, Oregon 97402

Verses marked NIV are taken from the Holy Bible: New International Version®. NIV®. Copyright © 1973, 1978, 1984 by the International Bible Society. Used by permission of Zondervan Publishing House. The "NIV" and "New International Version" trademarks are registered in the United States Patent and Trademark Office by International Bible Society.

Verses marked NASB are taken from the New American Standard Bible®, © 1960, 1962, 1963, 1968, 1971, 1972, 1973, 1975, 1977 by The Lockman Foundation. Used by permission.

Verses marked KJV are taken from the King James Version of the Bible.

Cover by Terry Dugan Design, Minneapolis, Minnesota

Published in association with the literary agency of Alive Communications, Inc., 7680 Goddard Street, Suite 200, Colorado Springs, CO 80920.

THE TREASURE INSIDE YOUR CHILD
Copyright © 2001 by Pam Farrel
Published by Harvest House Publishers
Eugene, Oregon 97402

Library of Congress Cataloging-in-Publication Data
Farrel, Pam, 1959–
        The treasure inside your child / Pam Farrel.
            p. cm.
        Includes bibliographical references.
        ISBN 0-7369-0605-3
            1. Parenting—Religious aspects—Christianity. 2. Children—Religious life. 3. Family—
        Religious life. I. Title.
BV4529.F38 2001
248.8'45—dc21   2001024263

Printed in the United States of America

01 02 03 04 05 06 07 08 09 10 /BC-PT/ 10 9 8 7 6 5 4 3 2 1

To the children who are a treasure to me:

My three wonderful sons, Brock, Zach, and Caleb.
Thank you for sharing your lives so other children
can discover the treasure God placed in them.
The verse I am praying for you three is,
"Be on your guard; stand firm in the faith;
be men of courage; be strong" (1 Corinthians 16:13).

And to my precious nieces and nephews:
Rebekah, Lora Kate, Jacob, Owen,
Gianna, Brad, Jill, Lindsay, and Kevin.
Your love is a treasure to me.

May each of you reach your
God-given potential
and live to please Jesus.

CONTENTS

For you created my inmost being;
you knit me together in my mother's womb.
I praise you because I am fearfully and wonderfully made;
your works are wonderful, I know that full well.
My frame was not hidden from you
when I was made in the secret place.
When I was woven together in the depths of the earth,
your eyes saw my unformed body.
All the days ordained for me were written in your book
before one of them came to be.

◆ ◆ ◆

Psalm 139:13-16

1

WHERE YOUR HEART IS

*Parenthood Is All About
a Treasure Hunt*

After months of endless anticipation Christmas Day finally arrived—my due date. Because I couldn't travel, my family came to me. All day long they looked at my protruding stomach and waited for labor to magically start. But it didn't. By the end of the day, I had come to grips with my first eye-opening parenting discovery: *I am not in control.*

Six days later, on New Year's Eve, my contractions came... and came and came. After nearly 20 hours of labor, with the nurse announcing I was only dilated to one centimeter and that the baby was in fetal distress, Brock was ushered into the world via an emergency C-section. Eye-opening discoveries two and three: *Parenting hurts* and *no one can ever explain just how much you will love your child.*

Mom had arrived two days before Christmas to help me for two weeks after the baby was born, but Brock's stubbornness about arriving on time had eaten up several of those days. So it happened that my wonderful mother, with all her wealth of practical wisdom and calm assurance, was being whisked out the door to the airport just over a week after we brought our new son home. About 2 A.M. that same night Brock woke up ready to eat. Bill had made the commitment to get the baby for these nightly feedings, so he brought Brock to me. I couldn't find a comfortable position to nurse in bed, so I went out to the living room to sit with my small soft bundle and pray.

Aaaaaaah God, this is exactly how I pictured motherhood. My baby looks so angelic resting upon my breast. I am looking forward to parenting Brock with such a great husband like Bill. He is so wise, so godly, such a good and gentle man—and handsome. I hope Brock will look like him and be like him. Life is so perfect...

As I rocked and talked to God, Brock finished nursing and fell asleep in my arms—for a few brief minutes. Then he started to cry. So I rocked him and burped him. But he kept crying. I walked with him and sang to him. And he kept crying. So I put him in the baby swing and he cried even louder. I took him back out, and in my heart I shouted to God an order: *God, You control the whole universe, can't You control this baby? Please make him quit crying!*

Brock kept crying.

I tried giving him a bottle of water—but he kept crying. I walked and I jiggled and I patted and he kept crying—and so did I. Here we were standing in the middle of a pitch-black room both sobbing our eyes out. I thought about waking up Bill, but I didn't think he would know what to do. He hadn't even baby-sat growing up. I thought about calling my mom. I knew she'd know what to do, but it was 4 A.M. I knew she would be fine if I called, but that would mean I'd have to own up to the real facts of the situation: *I have no idea what I am doing!*

I walked, patted, and sang every hymn and baby lullaby I could think of. I even made up a lullaby, hoping to get points for creative mothering. He still kept crying. Before this moment, I could never comprehend some of the tragic responses mothers had with the onset of the baby blues. I could never understand how emotions could get away from a person so much that they would shake a baby just to quiet him or her. But now I did understand, and that understanding frightened me. I was exhausted and overwhelmed. I only wanted the best for my baby, and I was afraid I didn't have what it took to give it.

Through tears I cried out again to God. *Lord, I know You can make Brock quit crying. You have the power, but I don't think that's what You want here. I admit I don't have a clue. Even though I read parenting books and attended classes for parents of newborns, I still don't know what to do. I've tried everything I know, so I guess I am asking for a miracle. I need Your wisdom. I have none of my own. God, please, please, please give me Your wisdom. I'm resting in You. I'm counting on You.*

Brock didn't instantly stop crying, but immediately I was filled with a peace that to this day I can't really describe with words. I didn't have the answer, but I felt assured an answer would come. I didn't have the presence of my mom, but the presence of God's Spirit was calming my own. As I relaxed, my body began to slow to a rhythmic sway. I didn't feel frantic anymore, so my pats on Brock's back gave way to a tender gentle circling motion. Soon my son was fast asleep.

I had known, intellectually, that I could depend on God, that He loved my son even more than I did, but now I was emotionally convinced as well. I decided that day to go to God first when I wondered what to do as a parent. I decided to take God up on His offer, "If any of you lacks wisdom, he should ask God, who gives generously to all without finding fault, and it will be given to him" (James 1:5). What a gracious God. I knew I could ask Him anything and I'd never hear, "What a stupid question!" or "I can't believe you can't figure this one out!"

I've seen Him orchestrate my schedule so I heard just the right show on the radio, sat at just the right table next to just the right mom who had gone through exactly what I was struggling with, or send a magazine on just the right day with just the right article in it. I've read verses in the Bible that seem to pop off the page with just the right perspective, and I've remembered just the right story from my own upbringing, or just the right new idea would pop into my mind at just the right time. The more I was committed to prayer, the more I saw God answer.

Bill and I are on a parenting journey. Like you, we are travelers on this road looking to bring out the best in our children, and we have discovered a map. God's Word and the principles in it can serve us all well. It is our hope that this book will serve as a compass to guide you to the treasure, that unique treasure, that God has prepared for you and your children.

The most important step is the first one. The Bible is a treasure map that must be read with the heart. To succeed on this treasure hunt we must prepare our own hearts to see the treasure in our children.

Desperate Parents Will Pray Desperate Things

Hannah desperately wanted a child. Her husband tried to help with words he thought were encouraging: "Hannah, why are you weeping? Why don't you eat? Why are you downhearted? Don't I mean more to you than ten sons?" (1 Samuel 1:8). That's like asking, "Isn't my love enough?" But it wasn't. Hannah wanted a baby. She went to the temple one day to pray. She didn't know what else to do, so she poured out her heart to God.

She must have been an emotional wreck because when Eli the priest saw her, he thought she was drunk. But she wasn't! She was honest, transparent, real, and in real need of an answer from God.

> In bitterness of soul Hannah wept much and prayed to the LORD. And she made a vow, saying, "O LORD Almighty, if you will only look upon your servant's misery and remember me, and not forget your servant but give her a son, then I will give him to the LORD for all the days of his life, and no razor will ever be used on his head."
>
> As she kept on praying to the LORD, Eli observed her mouth. Hannah was praying in her heart, and her lips were moving but her voice was not heard. Eli thought she was drunk and said to her, "How long will you keep on getting drunk? Get rid of your wine."
>
> "Not so, my lord," Hannah replied, "I am a woman who is deeply troubled. I have not been drinking wine or beer; I was pouring out my soul to the LORD. Do not take your servant for a wicked woman; I have been praying here out of my great anguish and grief."
>
> Eli answered, "Go in peace, and may the God of Israel grant you what you have asked of him."
>
> She said, "May your servant find favor in your eyes." Then she went her way and ate something, and her face was no longer downcast.
>
> Early the next morning they arose and worshiped before the LORD and then went back to their home at

Ramah. Elkanah lay with Hannah his wife, and the LORD remembered her. So in the course of time Hannah conceived and gave birth to a son. She named him Samuel, saying, "Because I asked the LORD for him" (1 Samuel 1:10-20).

In her prayer Hannah had promised something every parent should promise—to give our children back to God. We do not own our children. God has lent them to us, entrusted them to us, and our job as parents is to pass God's wisdom, God's perspective, and God's instruction on to them, all the while holding them with an openhanded attitude. This is the first skill we need. *They are Yours, God. Make me a good steward. Help me love them as You would. Help me parent them as You would. Make me more like You so they can see You and Your will clearly.*

Godly Parents Model Integrity

The second skill that will prepare our hearts to understand the map is integrity. My son Caleb has a keen memory. Anytime we even appear to have forgotten anything, Caleb will say, "You promised!" He knows we only promise if we intend on keeping our word. Because of that, we are very careful with what we have promised.

Hannah promised God she would give her son back to Him to serve in His temple. But think of how she must have felt, or how many ways she could have rationalized reneging on her word. She could have argued: *But look at all those other women with all those children. Can't You just use one of theirs?* or *But, God, I have only had him for a few years. Can't you wait until he is older—say 50?*

But Hannah kept her promise. She was a woman of integrity.

> She said to her husband, "After the boy is weaned, I will take him and present him before the LORD, and he will live there always."
>
> "Do what seems best to you," Elkanah her husband told her. "Stay here until you have weaned him; only may the LORD make good his word." So the woman stayed at home and nursed her son until she had weaned him.
>
> After he was weaned, she took the boy with her, young as he was, along with a three-year-old bull, an ephah of flour and a skin of wine, and brought him to the house of the LORD at Shiloh. When they had slaughtered the bull, they brought the boy to Eli, and she said to him, "As surely as you live, my lord, I am the woman who stood here beside you praying to the LORD. I prayed for this child, and the LORD has granted me what I asked of him. So now I give him to the LORD. For his whole life he will be given over to the LORD" (1 Samuel 1:22-28).

What was the outcome of Hannah's integrity?

Her son Samuel heard God's clear and personal call to the ministry when he was very young, and he went on to be one of the greatest judges in Israel's history, even being chosen to anoint kings, including King David.

The best gift Hannah gave her son was the example of integrity.

Character Counts

In parenting, more is caught than taught. The phrase, "Do as I say, not as I do" inevitably falls on deaf ears. In our

20 plus years of marriage and full-time pastoral ministry, Bill and I have discovered that if we could give all children one gift, we would give them a mom and dad who loved to worship and *obey* God. We have seen over and over how a breach of integrity causes trauma in a child's heart.

Trauma comes in all shapes and sizes. Run down the list below and see if your child has ever had:

- A parent who abuses drugs or alcohol
- A parent who is jailed for breaking a law
- A parent who is absent due to workaholism
- A parent who has abandoned the child
- A parent who is hooked on pornography
- A parent who is physically abusive
- A parent who is emotionally or verbally abusive
- A parent who is sexually abusive
- A parent who is chronically unemployed
- A parent who is no longer at home because of divorce
- A parent who has had an affair
- A parent who has once walked with God and now doesn't

If one of these situations has caused pain in your child's life, you will have a special challenge in front of you. Sin always causes trauma, but God can redeem and restore. If your child has suffered due to sin on your part, a spouse's, or because of another person, you will need to seek God diligently to redeem the trauma. *You can't go back, but you can go forward.* God is the master of turning dark into light, bad into good. He isn't just a pathfinder; He's a way-maker. He will go before you and your child if you partner with Him in parenthood with integrity.

Compare and Contrast

You have a choice. You could be known as a person like Timothy's mother and grandmother, whom the apostle Paul commended for passing the baton of faith well: "I have been reminded of your sincere faith, which first lived in your grandmother Lois and in your mother Eunice and, I am persuaded, now lives in you also" (2 Timothy 1:5).

Or you can also choose to parent in your own power and follow the example of Rebekah, who lied and manipulated her husband so that her favorite son would receive the blessing of the eldest son.

Timothy, even as a youth, was known as a godly leader. Rebekah's son Jacob had a life filled with strife. His own betrayed brother hated him so much that he had to run for his life! Then he was taken in by a lying and manipulating father-in-law, who tricked him into marrying the sister of the woman he loved. Jacob had to stay and work seven more years to gain the hand of Rachel (see Genesis 25–29). His story gives deeper meaning to what goes around, comes around or the biblical principle, you reap what you sow (Galatians 6:7).

You have a choice regarding what you will pass on as a legacy. It can be dysfunction and sin or health and holiness. Exodus 34:7 explains a principle of dysfunction: "Keeping mercy for thousands, forgiving iniquity and transgression and sin, and that will by no means clear the guilty; visiting the iniquity of the fathers upon the children, and upon the children's children, unto the third and to the fourth generation" (KJV).

This doesn't mean that God holds the sin of a grandparent against a grandchild yet unborn. Rather, it is a statement of fact: *Left unchecked, the sins of the father will be visited upon generation after generation.* The reason this is true is that if you grow up in an unhealthy family, love to you is expressed in unhealthy ways: yelling, chaos, one dramatic event after another, violence, rejection, and so on. Children who see dad hit mom, then make up with roses, will learn that love and pain go hand in hand. Unless they deliberately retrain themselves, they will choose to marry a person that will help them reestablish the pattern—even learning behavior patterns to push a person to say or do things that will feel painful. It is a horrible cycle, but Bill and I see it in family and marriage counseling on a weekly basis. Sin, when it is repeated generation after generation, looks normal. That's why you will see generation after generation of welfare mothers. Girls who had fathers who abused alcohol, drugs, and tobacco will often marry men who abuse. Patterns of lying, cheating, stealing, and divorce will show up in branch after branch of family trees.

But you can also pass on healthy patterns. A psalmist declares: "We will not hide them from their children; we will tell the next generation the praiseworthy deeds of the LORD, his power, and the wonders he has done...to teach their children, so the next generation would know them, even the children yet to be born, and they in turn would tell their children" (Psalm 78:4-6).

That is why you can also see generation after generation of pastors, missionaries, Christian leaders, and strong godly families. In my travels I have the privilege of meeting children and grandchildren of spiritual leaders whom I have looked up to in their writings, through their radio ministries, and in their biographies. When I ask them what it was like growing up in their family, they often make statements like, "It was normal to obey God" or "I can never remember a time when our whole family didn't pray in crisis or a Christmas that the Christmas story wasn't read." One woman, who was the sixth generation to be in full-time ministry, said, "I cannot imagine not having the strength of my heritage. When I encounter a problem in ministry, I can call my parents, my grandparents, aunts, uncles, brothers...I have so many that will pray for me and give me godly counsel." There is great strength in this kind of heritage.

A Redeemer and a Rebuilder

As a parent, if the breach of integrity is with you, you have the ability to repent and rebuild—and we've seen God do amazing things in rebuilding relationships, marriages, families, and children. I feel that I am a living, breathing example of how God can heal anyone and reparent us when one parent has fallen short.

I had a wonderful, creative, goal-setting, nurturing mother. I believe she took much of the trauma of our home. She often stood between me and the wrath and anger of my alcoholic father. When I came home from dates, I remember praying, begging God to not let my dad be passed out on the front lawn in his underwear, in an angry rage, or worse: suicidal.

When I was a preschooler, my mother had a friend, Kathy, who was a secretary of a little church in our small town. Mom noticed that Kathy had what she wanted— peace, joy, and patience. The fruit of the spirit emanated from Kathy's life. My mother began to attend Kathy's church, and always took my brother, my sister, and me to Sunday school. Mom would then go home, but I would beg to stay for "big church" (the worship service).

I felt so close to God in that beautiful sanctuary, always lit up with the colored rays of its stained glass windows. And I felt safe there. In Sunday school I earned a little white cross that glowed in the dark for memorizing the Twenty-Third Psalm. On it was printed, "He Lives." I remember one night, when I was just eight, as my dad raged and my mom tried to talk him down, I was lying on my bed and looking up at that little cross glowing in the dark. I prayed, *God, at church they tell me You had the power to rise from the dead. I believe You have the power to do anything. When I grow up, I don't want to live in a house like this with all this fighting. I want to live in a nice quiet house—like my pastor's. Lord, I think I'd like to marry a pastor.*

Shortly after that I was trying to earn a place on the quiz team at church. I always tried to earn any award I could because I thought that might make Dad happy, and then he might show he loved me. I was memorizing Matthew 5, 6, and 7 when I came across Matthew 7:7, "Ask and it will be given to you; seek and you will find; knock and the door will be opened to you." There, sitting on my bed, I prayed *God, does this mean if I ask You to come into my life, You will? Please come into my life and be my best friend, my Savior, and my Lord.*

I believe He met me there that day.

I began to be transformed from the inside out. I went from a sullen child who cried at the drop of a hat to a happy, carefree little girl. My circumstances didn't change—God was changing me. He was carrying out His promise to be a father to the fatherless (Psalm 68:5), and if my dad didn't want to do the job right, He would. I treated God just like a father, going to Him with everything in my life. I read His Word and talked to Him all day, every day.

God had a lot to remake in me: fear of rejection, fear of failure, and fear of men. And I could easily fall into controlling patterns because the home I grew up in felt out of control. As a teen I even went my own way for a while.

However, as I continued to look to Him as my father, He was faithful to continue to work with me. God led me to forgive my father, to look at my own weaknesses, and then as a young adult to look to Him as my strength.

I quit needing awards to validate myself, and this has freed me to pursue excellence just for the sheer joy of a job well done. When He finally had my full attention, God had me reevaluate all of my life—the way I chose men, the way I made decisions, how I dressed, and what activities I partook in. This new process freed me to choose a godly man about a year later. Our relationship and our family are dramatically different from the home I grew up in.

As a young mother, I continued to ask God to point out any unhealthy traits, any blind spots I might have due to the way I was raised. One example is that I felt a need to keep a perfect home, and I found myself spending all day every day picking up after my children, getting very little of anything else done, and feeling more and more resentful. The anger was always boiling right under the surface. Then one day in a quiet time, God pointed out that my resentment and anger would create children who would feel they had to be perfect, and it could set them up for rebellion against me and Him. I made a few choices that day that I believe were a turning point in my parenting:

- ◆ Put God first. I begin to give Him the first sane 20 minutes! I knew only He could keep my perspective and expectations realistic.
- ◆ Whisper instead of yell if I was frustrated. When I felt anger, I immediately took that anger to Jesus and asked, "What is the underlying fear?" Anger is just a symptom of a deeper issue—what is the issue?

- ◆ My home is a safe place, not a showplace. This one was especially difficult. I wanted my family to look forward to coming home and having friends over. I wanted to use our home for ministry, but where there are crowds there can be chaos—or at least clutter. I chose to only clean up first thing in the morning, right before dinner (sometimes during nap but more often a few minutes before Bill arrived home), and at bedtime. This made for happier children and a mom with healthier interests. I gained time for Bible study, friendships, art, exercise, and education.

- ◆ I taught myself to play a tape of truth—phrases of wisdom and portions of verses that gave me clarity when old patterns of control threatened my home front. I would tell myself things like, "Lighten up and live life. A quiet answer turns away wrath. The fruit of the spirit is love, joy, peace, patience...and self-control." I found if I had Christian radio or music on all day, we all had better days.

I know God can heal any trauma you or your child may have gone through. But it is WORK. As a part of my healing, I read many books, I was discipled, I sought out good counsel, and I spent nearly two years of my quiet times researching who God was so I could again see Him clearly and receive all that my heavenly Father had for me. God is continually pulling out issues from the closets of my life and then graciously says, *Ok, Pam, now let's work on repairing this one.*

God might open the closet of your life as a parent while you read this book. While the focus of the book will be your child, in learning tools to unlock the treasure in your son or daughter, you might come to grips with some of the short-comings of your own family. Give those hurts to God. He can help you go forward to create a new family that reflects all that He has to offer.

◆ ◆ ◆

"I KNOW, AND GOD KNOWS."

When I was first pregnant, even the first day Bill and I discovered I was to have a baby, we would lie in bed and Bill would place his hand on mine then place both our hands on my stomach and we'd pray. We prayed all the typical prayers first-time parents might pray: *Please make the baby healthy, help us be good parents, make this child a difference-maker in this world.* But Bill and I also prayed and asked God big things for our child:

God, give him or her the faith of a Daniel or a Joseph. Give him or her the courage to stand for You—even the courage to stand alone for You. Make him or her a strong witness of light in this dark world. May many come to know You personally because of the life of this little one.

Our prayer was beautifully answered over and over. When Brock was a sophomore, I drove into the school parking lot to pick him up. It was already dark, and all the players were off the field—everyone except my son who, like every day after practice, was voluntarily putting equipment away. I was in a rush so I ran to the field. "Brock, honey, I'm in a hurry. I have to run you home, feed you dinner, run you back for Student Venture, and get to a Bible study I have to teach."

"Ok, Mom, but I have to do repos." (Repos are these grueling exercises football players have to do up and down the field when they have done something wrong.)

"Why do you have to do repos? You *never* have to do repos."

"I didn't send my beg letter (fund raising letters)."

"They are sitting on my desk. They are all done, I just have to get stamps for them."

"Yeah, but they aren't sent."

"You're right. Do the repos."

I walked back up to the locker room. Brock's teammates were starting to come out.

"Hey, Mrs. Farrel! Where's Brock?"

I repeated the story to them. One said, "Man, I didn't send my beg letters either. But coach doesn't know that—and all the coaches are gone. No one would know."

Just then, Brock walked up, and he heard the conversation. "I'd know, and God knows." His choosing to be a person of integrity was a witness to his friends that day and warmed my heart.

2

AVOIDING FOOL'S GOLD

Four Things Your Children Would Rather Have than Real Treasure

I was a chaperone on Zachery's eighth-grade trip to the Mother Lode country. As a part of the trip, we spent an afternoon panning for gold—in the rain. It was cold outside. The water in the river felt as though the ice had been chipped off so we could dip our pans in it. We heard how miners would wade, sometimes up to their waists, in the frigid water to find a place that had yet to be panned. It was a laborious process. Scoop up a bunch of bedrock, swirl it around in the pan just right so the bigger rocks washed off and the smaller stayed, add water, and swish over and over and over again until only the smallest of pebbles—and hopefully nuggets of gold—remained. Then, if you were fortunate enough to find any gold nuggets, you would have to take them sometimes a great distance to have them weighed.

You could trade them for money, or if you wanted, you could also become a goldsmith who would heat up the gold, melting it until the dross or impurities would rise to the surface. You'd repeat this process over and over until you could see your own reflection in it. Then you had pure gold! The process of panning to purification was arduous, time-consuming, and back-breaking—just as parenting is a time-consuming, often heart-wrenching task. But the results are the same. Nothing feels more rewarding than to shout, "Eureka! I've found pure gold!"

Children are innocent but they come to us with a bent for bad. The Bible is clear: "All have sinned" (Romans 3:23). No one has to teach a child to be selfish—that comes prepackaged. Over our years in ministering to children, teens, and their families, we have observed four traits that can lead children to destruction. Every child we have ever met has at least one, some more than that, and these traits must be minimized in order for your child to discover and then live out the God-given treasure and calling He has planned. It is one of our main jobs as parents to heat up life so that the dross of the negative bents our children have can rise to the surface, be dealt with, and then eliminated. The four negative traits we see entrap individuals most are: sensuality, rebellion, shortsightedness, and laziness. These are things your child might prefer over real gold.

Sensuality

Samson was special from the womb. He took a Nazirite vow which set him apart as a holy leader. But he had a fatal flaw. In Judges 14:1-3, we see a snapshot of his sensual side.

Samson went down to Timnah and saw there a
young Philistine woman. When he returned, he said to
his father and mother, "I have seen a Philistine woman
in Timnah; now get her for me as my wife."

His father and mother replied, "Isn't there an
acceptable woman among your relatives or among all
our people? Must you go to the uncircumcised Philistines to get a wife?"

But Samson said to his father, "Get her for me.
She's the right one for me."

Judges 16:1 also indicates that Samson had difficulty
with his sensuality, "One day Samson went to Gaza, where
he saw a prostitute. He went in to spend the night with her."

You may be familiar with Delilah, the beautiful woman
who used her sensuality and beauty to pry the secret to
Samson's strength from him. Repeatedly Delilah asked
Samson the secret to his strength, and he would make up an
answer. Then she would yell, "The Philistines are upon
you!" Then out would jump soldiers in waiting, who would
try to capture Samson, the strongest man in the nation.

Logic would say, "Samson, get out of there. This woman
is no good for you! She is using you! She's willing to sell you
out!" But he was ensnared by his own sensual sin. He was
addicted to sensuality even at the risk of his own life. Delilah
finally pulled the secret to his strength out of him. One
fateful evening, his hair was cut and his strength dimin-
ished. He was bound and then pitifully blinded.

One way to discern if sensuality is a weakness is looking
for a child's interest in the opposite sex. How much does he
or she focus on body parts? How does he or she respond to
sexually slanted commercials and print ads? Undue interest
at a young age is often a flashing yellow light.

Because of our position in the church, we see many accidents waiting to happen. On more than one occasion, we have observed very young girls of eight and nine wanting to wear makeup, dress provocatively, and place themselves in inappropriate positions with older boys and grown men. A resounding alarm should ring if you see a preteen or young teen sitting on laps, rubbing her body against boys and men, or dressing to arouse. Your senses should tingle if your preadolescent son is overly interested in or is eating up the ego-stroking attention of the opposite sex at the sacrifice of other more vital interests.

If you notice preteens or teens losing their direction or purpose, this is a serious storm warning. One teen told me, "This guy at school came right up to me. I don't even know him and he said, 'Do you want to have sex?' I know I should be revolted. But instead I wanted to say yes. It makes me feel so sexy and so loved that he is attracted to me that way." However, regardless of feelings, the truth is that those who are unwilling to rein in their sensual side will be forced to live out the painful consequences of their choices.

Rebellion

One of the hardest type of child to parent is the rebellious child. First Samuel 2:12-16 gives an example of a godly leader who raised his children to know right from wrong, but the sons didn't want to do what was right!

> Eli's sons were wicked men; they had no regard for the LORD. Now it was the practice of the priests with the people that whenever anyone offered a sacrifice and while the meat was being boiled, the servant of the priest would come with a three-pronged fork in his

hand. He would plunge it into the pan or kettle or caldron or pot, and the priest would take for himself whatever the fork brought up. This is how they treated all the Israelites who came to Shiloh. But even before the fat was burned, the servant of the priest would come and say to the man who was sacrificing, "Give the priest some meat to roast; he won't accept boiled meat from you, but only raw."

If the man said to him, "Let the fat be burned up first, and then take whatever you want," the servant would then answer, "No, hand it over now; if you don't, I'll take it by force."

Rebellious kids have a bent toward evil. They sometimes dabble in Satanism, they can lie to your face, and they may boldly disrespect authority or passive-aggressively tell you what you want to hear and then do the opposite. They often show signs of violence early in life. They may torture animals, treat peers cruelly, or say hateful things for more than just a "phase." Every child will have periods in his or her life when disobedience is close to the surface, but the rebellious child will display a consistent pattern of nonobedience and argumentativeness.

Shortsightedness

Genesis 25:29-34 shares a story of one very shortsighted choice:

Once when Jacob was cooking some stew, Esau came in from the open country, famished. He said to Jacob, "Quick, let me have some of that red stew! I'm famished!" (That is why he was also called Edom.)

Jacob replied, "First sell me your birthright."

"Look, I am about to die," Esau said. "What good is the birthright to me?"

But Jacob said, "Swear to me first." So he swore an oath to him, selling his birthright to Jacob.

Then Jacob gave Esau some bread and some lentil stew. He ate and drank, and then got up and left.

So Esau despised his birthright.

Esau had the world by the tail. He was to be the leader of his family, which meant that he was also to be the CEO of a great empire. But he was hungry, so to meet a short-term desire, he gave away the most valuable asset he owned—his birthright.

These kids just don't think life through. A shortsighted teen will bring a knife to a zero-tolerance school just to show his friends how cool it is. A shortsighted child will wander off because he wanted to see what was on the other side of the hill. A shortsighted boy is angry so he slugs his friend, expelling himself from school. A shortsighted girl may go off with friends without calling home because it didn't even cross her mind that others might worry. These kids aren't manipulative or rebellious, they just act stupid at times. They have an inability to see the long-term results of their actions.

Laziness

When Brock was nine, his bike was stolen from our front yard. He came in crying, "Mom, my bike is missing. Do you think someone stole it?"

"Honey, there is a good chance that someone might have taken it. We need to pray for that person and ask God to reach his or her heart. God makes all things right in the end. He is a fair judge."

A few weeks later, a young man who had been attending church with a friend for several months needed a place to stay. He was homeless, and my husband was working on getting him into a long-term drug rehabilitation program. He was off drugs (or so we thought), and he wanted a fresh start in life. We asked the kids if he could spend a night or two until he could get into the program. Brock volunteered to give up his room and his bed.

Program after program was full, and Jerry's name was added to waiting list after waiting list. He didn't have a job, so we made a contract he was to abide by while he stayed. Just like any member of the family, he would have chores too. I would start all my boys and Jerry on their chores in the morning, and my seven- and nine-year-old children would work Jerry under the table! I was forever getting him up off the sofa, reminding him to finish tasks, and urging him to keep working toward his simple goals. Jerry was smart. At one time he had an academic scholarship for college. But his laziness lost that scholarship. Then his laziness lost him job after job. His laziness got him kicked out of one friend's home after another.

One day he asked me if he could use my bike to ride to a friend's and pick up some of his belongings so he'd have them for when he entered Teen Challenge a few days later. I let him, and I was actually rejoicing because I thought at least he had to pedal! He didn't come home that night. I thought we'd never see him again—but we did. The next day he came walking in—minus my bike. It seems Jerry fell asleep at his friend's house while his friend stole my bike and sold it for drugs. Jerry slept on the floor of our church that night, not in Brock's bed. Laziness was not going to be rewarded by me or modeled before my sons any longer. The next day Bill drove him four hours north to Teen Challenge. (Teen Challenge is an amazing organization that helps young adults get off drugs and alcohol.) Jerry thanked us and we prayed. We saw him go with heavy hearts. We knew his single, drug-addicted mom felt prostitution was more important than teaching her son values, but we also knew Jerry had gone through a string of good people extending a helping hand. His laziness lost him opportunity after opportunity.

Weeding the Garden

How can a parent work to eliminate the negative and accentuate the positive? *Discipline.* What is discipline?

Let's look to God's Word and see what principles we can pull from Scripture:

Verse: He will die for lack of discipline, led astray by his own great folly (Proverbs 5:23).

Principle: If a parent does not discipline, there is an increased probability of a child being led into something much worse of his own accord.

Verse: Discipline your son, and he will give you peace; he will bring delight to your soul (Proverbs 29:17).

Principle: The outcome of a disciplined child is a child who will give you peace and bring delight to you.

Verse: "I am with you and will save you," declares the LORD..."I will discipline you but only with justice; I will not let you go entirely unpunished" (Jeremiah 30:11).

Principle: God disciplines with justice. He doesn't let wrong go unpunished, but neither is He unfair.

Verse: No discipline seems pleasant at the time, but painful. Later on, however, it produces a harvest of righteousness and peace for those who have been trained by it (Hebrews 12:11).

Principle: It will not feel pleasant to give or receive discipline, but the outcome of righteous living and peace will feel good.

Verse: Those whom I love I rebuke and discipline. So be earnest, and repent (Revelation 3:19).

Principle: The right response or outcome to discipline will be a desire to earnestly obey and a repentant heart.

First Things First

From these verses, one can conclude that discipline is not only necessary but also has a positive outcome. Let's look briefly at some specific components of appropriate discipline:

Training first. You cannot punish for something the person didn't know was wrong. To do so would be unjust, and God's model is discipline that is just. Irresponsibility should never be punished unless it is deliberate and defiant. Children are naturally clumsy and immature. It is for this very reason they need to be trained and instructed by adults. A child should never be made to feel guilty for being a child, and yet too often parents use discipline to respond to "spilled milk."

The punishment should fit the offense. A small infraction should be met with a small form of correction. A big wrongdoing should be met with a more stringent form of correction.

A person worthy of honor should give the discipline. The parent who was there at the time of the infraction is best. And the discipline will probably be better received if you as a parent are living according to God's principles.

Discipline includes physical correction. Physical punishment in the form of a rod of correction is permissible and even recommended in Scripture.

Correct in control. No punishment, correction, or discipline should ever be given in anger.

The Controversy Continues

To spank or not to spank? Good parents line up on both sides of this issue, and so do bad parents. People's emotions often run high when discussing spanking. No loving person would ever want a child to be abused, but in the same way no loving person would want a parent to let children run totally according to their own whims and rules. A swing of the pendulum in either direction is off balance.

Regardless of the form of discipline, I believe it isn't just what discipline we use but how we use it and why we use it that matters. Bill and I prayed about and discussed all forms of discipline while I was pregnant. We decided we would never spank in anger and we'd never hurl cutting words or dole out consequences if we were angry. We'd pray and make sure our emotions were in check and settled first. We both had grown up with a parent who cut to the quick with hurtful words. Hurtful words said in anger cause damage rather than correction. We agreed to take words like *"stupid"* and all its synonyms out of our vocabulary. We made a commitment to use corporal punishment (spanking) for a very limited number of infractions.

As we looked at the teens in our youth group, the kids who were excelling all respected their parents' authority. They had a deep level of trust for their parents' overall wisdom even when they disagreed with the punishment at the time. I did an informal survey. All of the kids that were excelling as teens had been spanked at least a few times during their preschool years, and a few up until about first or second grade. Bill and I decided we wanted to protect our children from worse consequences by using spanking to lay out a few key boundaries.

When our boys were toddlers and preschoolers and they would do something that might endanger their lives, or the lives of their siblings, they would receive a spanking. For example, running into the street or playing with matches was an offense that called for corporal punishment.

The other offense we punished with spanking was flat out defiant disobedience. This wasn't when they just did something we asked them not to, but when it was accompanied with an attitude and often the words, "No, Mommy!" or "Stupid Daddy!" We knew we had to win the battle of respect when they were four or we'd never win it at 14.

Combining Discipline

I have found that the more strong-willed the child is, the more creative and layered your discipline will need to be. You will need to attack a sinful pattern of disobedience from all sides. When Zach was four, we were working at the new property where we were building our home. The house had been framed and the roof was on, but there were no walls yet. Just the framing of the rooms was in place. Zach loved sweets, but they added to his already hyperactive nature, so I restricted his intake. I found if I limited his sugar intake, he just got into less trouble.

However, he had discovered that we had an ice chest full of soda, chocolate, and other goodies for the volunteer workers. Zach would play, then sneak in and look around for witnesses. Thinking he saw none, he'd grab some goodies and flee. I spotted his antics and forbade him from having anymore before dinner. Then I saw him, as did Bill, as we were working in the next room (there were no walls, but Zach somehow thought that because he entered through a doorway, that we couldn't see him in the next room!).

He had the ice chest open. "Zach, get out of there right now!"

He had a ring of chocolate around his mouth. It was a new ring because I had just moments before wiped dirt and chocolate grime from his face. So I asked, "Zach, did you get more goodies out of the ice chest?"

Because he couldn't talk, he shook his head no. His cheeks were too stuffed with chocolate to respond.

"Zach, tell me the truth. Did you eat more chocolate after I told you not to?"

Again he shook his head no and then tried hard to swallow all the chocolate treasure he had in his little mouth.

"Zach, if you tell me the truth you won't get in as much trouble as you will if you lie to me. Did you eat more chocolate?"

Then Brock piped in, "You did too. Just tell them."

"Brock, this is between Zach and me. You go outside and play."

Zach shook his head no. In fact, his whole body shook in a back and forth "no" motion!

Bill stepped in. "Son, your mother and I saw you take and eat chocolate just now. Give it up. Own up to what you've done and it'll be better for you."

Again Zach shook his body "no!"

"Zach, because you disobeyed and then lied, Mommy has to spank you."

I took him to another room, and prayed with him, giving him one last chance to repent. Again, he defiantly shook his body "no." I then gave one swat to his bottom. I looked him eye to eye.

"Zach, Mommy loves you, but she has to be able to trust you. I need you to tell me the truth. Did you take more chocolate?"

This time he shouted, "No!" and stomped his little foot.

"Zach, I have to spank you for lying. Lying is the worst sin. It makes it so people can't trust you because they don't know if you are lying or telling the truth. Did you take the chocolate?"

"No!" he shouted in my face so loudly I could smell his chocolate breath!

"Zach, because you are lying to me, I have to spank you." Again I swatted his little bottom.

Then Bill tried to coerce a confession out of him. Then I tried again. Over and over we ask and pleaded with him to tell the truth. We prayed with him, hoping God's Spirit would help work on his cold, stony heart. Each time he lied. We knew just spanking was not getting through to him. He was determined to outlast us.

Finally, I carried him to the small travel trailer we had on the property. I sat him on the bed and said, "Zach, Mommy, Daddy, Brock, and God all saw what you did. We also know that you are lying about it. You will stay here and think about what happens when you lie." I told him the story of the boy who cried wolf and that when the real wolf came no one believed him. Then I reminded him of his Pinocchio book—that Pinocchio's nose grew every time he lied. I said, "Your nose would be out to here, son, if that were a true story, but it is just make-believe. But the truth of this is that we can't trust you when you lie. So you will have to stay here in this trailer until we go home tonight. Then tomorrow, when we return to work on the house, you won't be able to run and play. You will have to sit here in this trailer. Because if we can't trust you to obey us in the little things, like what is good for you to eat, then we can't trust you around all these tools and workers. Because you can't obey Mom and Dad, you will have to stay here in this trailer. You will have to stay here until you decide to tell us the truth about what you did today." I then prayed over him and asked God to lead him into all truth. I left him alone while I sat just out of sight on the steps of the trailer. At least an hour went by.

Finally, Zach peeked his head out of the door, and said through sobs of tears, "Mommy, I am sorry. I took the candy. I lied. Please forgive me."

I thanked him, told him I forgave him, and we prayed and hugged and went to get Daddy. "Daddy, I am sorry. I took it. I lied. I am sorry." His whole little body was shaking. The tears of repentance seemed like they were coming from his toes. It was dark, well past suppertime. We were all exhausted. Keeping Zach on the straight and narrow had taken hours out of our day. I bundled him up in my arms, and we all went to get dinner. Before we were a block away, he was sound asleep. His face shown like an angel. Peace once again reigned over his heart and mind. That was one of the last spankings we had to give him because we noticed that word pictures, stories, and separating him from the action had a greater impact than the pain of the spanking.

Because he was such a rough-and-tumble little boy, physical pain meant next to nothing to him. He could tough out any physical pain. But he lived to be part of the action, so time-outs were now working better.

However, early on, time-outs were not always easy to enforce and didn't work well with Zach. He was so strong-willed he wouldn't stay where you put him. I had to literally stand and hold him into the tiny time-out chair. The more he struggled, the longer the time-out would last. I had to choose well when to send him into a time-out because Zach's size and physical strength were exhausting me.

I found I had better results when I would sit him on my lap in the rocker. "Zach, we have to take a time-out. You are out of control, and you could hurt yourself or your brother so we are going to sit still in this rocker together until you calm down." Then I'd hold him close to me, and rock back and forth. The more he'd struggle, the tighter I would hug him. I would whisper in his ear, "Mommy loves you, and she wants what is best for you. You need to calm down and let your arms and legs rest. They have taken you into trouble, and we need them to not do that anymore. So let's sit together and rock and I'll sing and pray. We'll ask God to help you calm down."

So we'd sit and rock, and I'd sing and pray in quiet whispers. Sometimes it would take nearly an hour to calm him down. If he was defiant and would talk back then he'd get a spanking first, then the time-out.

Zach had many of the signs of ADD or hyperactivity, but Bill and I wanted to see if we could control it with diet, structure, and good parenting before we tried any medicine. It took a lot of energy on our part and a lot of creativity, but Zach did learn self-control. We found that if we wore him out physically each day, he was also easier to parent, so much of every day Zach spent outdoors playing, or at the park, and as soon as he was old enough, we had him in sports, where he not only tired himself out, he excelled. He began to feel great about himself. We also discovered humor worked well on him when he was just being rowdy but not defiant.

If he was just grumpy and out of sorts, I'd scoop him up and say, "Do we need to shake the ickies out of you? Are they hiding in your fingers" (then I'd jiggle his fingers) "or are they hiding in your toes?" (then I'd jiggle his toes). We'd make our way through each body part, and he'd giggle with glee. When I'd set him down, he'd be happy and obedient a little longer. I learned this trick from a mentor mom, a dear grandmother, who had baby-sat Brock. She did it for me one day as we walked Brock to the car. He was not wanting to go and it changed his mood so dramatically I logged it into my mom checklist to try before I resorted to more drastic discipline measures.

I decided to make a mental checklist each time before I disciplined:

- *Is this my problem or my child's?* Sometimes what they were asking was just an inconvenience, not defiance on their part. I was just preoccupied or not feeling well. No child should ever be punished for a parent's mood swings. I found I received more compliance if I was honest with my kids. "Honey, I'm sorry we can't do that right now. Mommy has a really bad headache. Let me take my medicine and let's lie on my bed. You can look at books, and I will rest my eyes. Then maybe later this afternoon, when I am feeling better, we can do that."

◆ *What is the simplest answer that will keep the boundary or rule that is in place?* When they were young, simply giving them another toy or another game to play with as a distraction often worked. Sometimes humor worked, like the "shake the ickies out" game or the "Rice Krispies" game. This game is great when you catch a child ready to break a rule but hasn't yet. I'd say, "Oh, no! It looks like Caleb needs an operation! He wants to do something wrong, but we can just take that desire out. Let's see, cut him open" (I'd pretend to cut him open by tickling him on his tummy in a straight line). "Ok, now let's pour in the Rice Krispies. Let's pour in the milk" (pretend to pour). "Snap, crackle, pop, snap, crackle, pop!" I'd tickle his tummy as I said those words until he would squeal in delight. It would usually break the mood or train of thought so I could start him on another activity.

◆ *Can I reason with him?* If children will listen to reason and turn their attention, it is always preferable. But young children often find reason to be an unwelcome guest in their world. Early in preschool, reasoning doesn't get their attention very well because they just can't cognitively understand cause and effect in abstract form.

◆ *Does she feel penned in?* Can I offer choices and still get compliance? By giving children choices, there are fewer showdowns. I want my children to be dressed for school, but almost anything in their closet is ok. I want them to eat breakfast, so leftover pizza is just as valid as scrambled eggs. Sometimes children rebel because they feel they are being turned into clones of their parents. Real discipline helps them be the best "them" God can make them.

◆ *Is this more of an issue of immaturity than defiance?* If it was immaturity, say boredom because the rest of the group is older and can do an activity but Mr. Two-Year-Old is bored and causing everyone else's fun to be ruined, then I would simply choose an alternative. If they have a tantrum over all the alternative options, I'd give a time-out. I had a rule of thumb, *If in doubt, give a time-out.* I knew if it truly was a defiant behavior, things would pretty much always get worse, so time was usually a great attitude indicator.

◆ *Is this defiance or a dangerous situation that would warrant a spanking?* If it did warrant a spanking, then we did it privately, never in front of others. We always explained the infraction fully, looking them eye to eye and having them repeat back our explanation to make sure they understood why they were being corrected.

◆ *Are there natural consequences that would make a longer-lasting impact?* Is this a privilege to be removed? What would happen if he were older? Can we mirror a consequence that might happen later in life? (Like if you break a window you have to earn the money to replace it.) We have found natural consequences work very well. We look to restrict their favorite activity: no TV, no friends over, no going to friends. But we didn't just take away, we added: "Since you can't get along with your brother, there will be no TV tonight, and instead you may go clean your room." I learned a lot from my close relationship with my grandparents. It seemed all the unruly teenage boys in the extended family would always be sent to spend a summer working on my grandfather's farm. If the boys snuck out and partied and drank the night away, Grandpa would just wake them up earlier and have more chores and more physically demanding chores for them to do. "Just keep 'em tired and they won't have the energy to get in trouble." As our own children got older and they would want to bow out of a social responsibility or a family activity we'd say, "Sure you can stay home, but here's the list of things that need to be done by the time we get back." It was amazing how fast the family activity looked like a good option!

Years before we had kids, we heard Dr. James Dobson say the goal of discipline was to shape the will without breaking the spirit. We thought that was a very worthy goal. In our discipline we try to always ask ourselves, "Is this shaping the will without breaking the spirit?" Boundaries and structure help children turn self-centeredness into God-centeredness and other-consciousness. A child who has been raised with consistent discipline and structure actually gains the most needed tool for success—self-mastery. Any person who can and will do what is right whether or not they may feel like doing it, has a head start over the rest of society.

◆　◆　◆

A FAMILY FORUM ON DISCIPLINE

Give each child one or more of the verses below on discipline and ask them the same question: Why is it good to take the discipline God, or God through your parents, gives you?

> The fear of the LORD is the beginning of knowledge, but fools despise wisdom and discipline (Proverbs 1:7).

> For these commands are a lamp, this teaching is a light, and the corrections of discipline are the way to life (Proverbs 6:23).

> He who heeds discipline shows the way to life, but whoever ignores correction leads others astray (Proverbs 10:17).

> He who ignores discipline comes to poverty and shame, but whoever heeds correction is honored (Proverbs 13:18).

> Buy the truth and do not sell it; get wisdom, discipline and understanding (Proverbs 23:23).

3

MORE PRECIOUS THAN SILVER

The Quest for Character

I sat in the rocker and nursed my beloved firstborn. He was just a few months old when we moved back to my hometown to become youth pastors in our home church. As I rocked back and forth, I thought of what the world might be like when my son would be a young adult. Things were rapidly going downhill in the culture. Drug use was on the rise. Suicide was the leading cause of death among teenagers, and in a close second were alcohol-related deaths. There were rumors of a new deadly disease that spread through sexual contact even as television and movie stars marched to make wrong right. As a new mother, I was overwhelmed at the thought my innocent son would have to someday grow up and face the world, perhaps a very corrupt world, maybe even as dark and far from God as Sodom and Gomorrah had been. I shuddered at the thought.

Then I prayed, and God's Spirit reminded me that I was not the only mother to pray such a prayer. One such mom had a son during the time Pharaoh was killing all male children because he feared the people he had enslaved would grow more numerous and stronger than his own people and would someday overthrow his bondage. Jochebed could keep her son quiet by nursing as the soldiers spread through the streets, searching house to house, but soon he would be too big. His cries of hunger would be too loud to muffle with the milk from her breasts. What then? "What can I do to save my son?" she must have cried out to the Lord.

An ingenious plan unfolded in her mind. She would take a basket, a basket she had woven with her own hands, and cover it with pitch to make it waterproof. She would place the baby in it, lay it in the bulrushes of the river Nile, and pray no one would find him. She prepared for the day and instructed Moses' older sister, Miriam, to place the baby in the basket and follow it should it move down the river. The basket did drift, and Miriam must have prayed in panic as she saw it heading directly to the palace steps where the princess, daughter of the Pharaoh, bathed. The princess directed her maidens to draw the basket from the river and was delighted to find a tiny baby inside.

Quickly thinking (and probably still praying), Miriam spoke out to the princess in a reverent whisper and arranged for a wet nurse for the baby. Miriam ran home, fetching her own mother to nurse her child in safety. As a wet nurse, Jochebed was given protection and privilege. As Pharaoh's son, Moses was given the best the world had to offer. Jochebed knew God had given her these precious years, brief but strategic, to prepare him to be a man of God within the palace walls. But what could a mother say? What could she teach? How much could she really impart in such a short amount of time?

My mind reeled as I thought about how Jochebed must have prayed, "God, give me wisdom. Give me discernment, clarity, to know what I should say, what I should sing, what I should pray, what I should teach and how I should teach it."

Four Key Areas to Develop

I had diligently searched through many books and many libraries to find out how long Moses and his mother were together. The commentators ranged from a few years to maybe five to seven years as the norm for nursing. One commentator said that in a few Eastern cultures, the wet nurse was kept on hand until a young man entered puberty, but most thought that weaning happened before the preschool years were complete.

I thought, *What would I teach, what would I sing and say and pray if I knew I'd only have five years to influence Brock?* Then I thought about the teens my husband and I worked with in ministry. *Lord, it seems as though some have what it takes to soar while others stumble when they turn 18. What's the difference? What character traits, what relationship and life skills, what spiritual skills do those who succeed have at 18 that give them the strength and courage to step out well into their calling?* I made a list of four key areas with the headings: Spiritual Skills, Relational Skills, Life Skills, and Character Qualities.

I began to brainstorm words and phrases under each heading. I tried to picture what priorities I'd have for Brock as he entered into the adult world. There were some things I knew he could learn after he left my influence, but I also realized there were many things he must learn before he ever left home. I decided to focus first on the skills and character qualities he would need to have strongly in place before he was a teen:

Spiritual Skills

How to love God
How to pray
How to share your faith
How to prepare a Bible lesson
How to lead a discussion group
How to disciple another
How to walk in the power of the Holy Spirit
How to handle temptation
How to obey God
How to follow and lead
How to choose a church
How to discern your spiritual gift
How to develop a servant's attitude
How to learn basic doctrine, theology, and church history

Character Qualities

Honesty	*Courage*
Fortitude	*Contentment*
Initiative	*Insightfulness*
Neatness	*Resourcefulness*
Compassion	*Flexiblity*
Empathy	*Creativity*
Loyalty	*Humility*
Integrity	

Relational Skills

Conversational skills	*Social graces*
Manners	*Respect for the opposite sex*
Mediation	*Respect for authority*
Delegation	*Respect for elders*

Life Skills

How to take care of personal belongings
How to care for a home
How to care for a pet
How to care for a car
How to save money
How to interview for a job
How to earn more responsibility, advance in career
How to balance a checkbook
How to be a lifelong learner
How to make appointments with medical and legal professionals
How to drive
How to use public transportation, travel, and tip
How to survive in an emergency or in the wilderness
How to use basic technology: radio, stereo, camera, computer
How to cook and clean

You may copy the "By the Time You Are 18" worksheet on the next page for your own use with each of your children.

By the Time You Are 18

Character Qualities

Relational Skills

Spiritual Skills

Life Skills

Tools of the Trade

One of the most important ways to build these character traits in each of your children is by providing a well-rounded education. Your children are growing up in an intellectually driven information age. If they are to find their place, they must be well prepared with the basics of language, writing, reading, math, history, and critical thinking. To accomplish this goal, there are many choices a parent must make for a child in the area of education.

There are three major choices a parent can use to educate a child: public school, private school (both secular and religious), and homeschool or independent learning. Bill and I have been in ministry for over 20 years and have seen godly Christians who have used any one, or a combination of choices, to achieve the goal. We do not believe one choice is necessarily more spiritual than the others. Rather, each year, for each child, parents should reevaluate what schooling option will best help a child accomplish the primary goals on the "By the Time You Are 18" worksheet while also instilling the basics of education.

Instead of telling you *what* to choose, I would rather give principles on *how* to choose which is best for your child at any given time. The benefits and drawbacks we have seen in each system of learning are listed on the next several pages.

Child Care Choices

Let's start with child care decisions, which begin the moment a baby is born.

Here are some facts to consider about that choice:

Science has shown that children gain more confidence and security later in life if they have bonded to one primary infant caretaker.[1] So the question isn't, "Do I work?" but rather, "How can I become a primary caretaker? How can I ensure a stable beginning and a secure bonding with this child I brought into this world?"

Toddlers and preschoolers have a need for a safe environment, freedom to learn, and a small social circle. Selma Frailberg, while a professor at the University of Michigan, discovered that children under three fared best when cared for by mother, while those three to six years of age could sustain absence from mother for half a day, but didn't tolerate well a prolonged absence of 10 to 12 hours.[2] The question then becomes, "How can I best see that these needs are met? And how do I decide when and if a child under five should have care other than parental care?"

Are my motives for wanting to work outside the home centered on God? (Both mom and dad should ask this question of themselves.) We can easily fall into the trap of working to fulfill needs *God* wants to meet in our life—needs of acceptance, camaraderie, and independence (rather than more healthy interdependence on one another or dependence on God). Or if we are honest, some of us know that when we look at ourselves squarely in the mirror we want to work to meet ego needs, like the power that comes from financial success, a title, or the ability to order others around. Are you ready to sacrifice your child's interests to secure your own?

And yet, if your basic expenses exceed your income, a second income may legitimately be needed. In those circumstances, how can you still choose what is best for your marriage and family?

First ask, is there any way to have a second income and still have one parent at home with the child? There are many at-home business opportunities in today's world that may be a possibility. Some marriages can survive tag-team parenting, some cannot. It is NOT in the best interest of the child if a couple is feeling the estrangement of no time together and is tempted to get their emotional and physical needs met outside the marriage. It is NOT in the best interest of the child if a tag-team child care arrangement leads to a divorce. But it is also NOT in the best interest of the child for bills to go unpaid on a regular basis.

If you have exhausted all options of a family-owned business, an entrepreneurial opportunity, or telecommuting, then other child care options must be considered. If so, ask these questions:

Is there a family member who is available for child care who would be a positive role model, and who would love our child(ren) the way we do? Sometimes grandma or grandpa, a sibling, or an aunt or uncle would welcome a day or two a week with a child.

Is there a homelike environment that comes with high credentials or high recommendations? This could mean care in your own home or care in a home day care. The smaller number of children cared for, the more like a family home setting it will be.

Some early child care options truly do provide well for the social, educational, and emotional well-being of a preschooler. However, these are not easy to find. The weight of a decision needs to be on who is doing the recommending or accrediting, what the long-term fruit of the care has been, and how much the child care provider is willing to raise your child(ren) the way you would raise them. To have a successful experience, the provider must be willing to be a teammate with you, the parent.

Is my child ready for a more formal child care setting? There are many preschool options. When choosing a preschool, a parent needs to have many safety assurances: Is the building safe and clean? How long have the staff been employed?

(Quick turnover is not a good sign.) What are the credentials of the teaching staff? Of the school itself? Can you contact other parents to get their opinion? Is the instructional style one which agrees with your parenting style? For example, Montessori preschools may be more open to child-led learning and taking advantage of teachable moments. Other preschools are more regimented and scheduled. Some provide many learning options like outdoor play, art, music, and spiritual education, while others provide only the basics of writing or math. The only way to know is to visit each school and stay for a while and observe. Are they open to part-time care at your choice of hours based upon your needs? What is the cost? (It is not always the most expensive that is the very best, but it is also true that you do get what you pay for.) Would you be seeking a preschool option even if child care weren't the issue? For example, parents of an only child or parents where children have large spaces in age will often seek out other children as playmates to enhance the development of social skills. Others want to make sure their child is ready for kindergarten, and they seek preschool hours for their child to accomplish that goal.

Each of my own sons was a part of preschool-like settings, but they were accomplished in different ways. Brock received wonderful preschool instruction once a week while I attended a Bible study through Bible Study Fellowship. Zach received great loving care two mornings a week after he was age four at a friend's home day care while I took a class to complete my education. Caleb, when he was four, attended a church-run preschool two mornings a week while I wrote. Each time, the major factor in the decision was our personal trust of the person(s) that would be directly relating to our son.

School Daze

When making the decision for education, keep these factors in mind. These lists are not exhaustive, but may provide a beginning point for your own evaluation of your options.

Public School

Strengths

- Probably attending with neighborhood children so a close neighborhood feeling for the family can develop
- Credentialed teachers with a four-year plus post-graduate education
- Strict regulations on backgrounds of staff
- Opportunity to witness for Christ, influence others to come to faith in Christ
- May provide special services to developmentally challenged or excelling children
- Some also have extras like libraries, computer labs, and science labs
- Higher pay can attract better educators
- No additional cost because taxes fund the school
- Parents can work during school hours. Some schools might offer after-school options

Weaknesses

- Cannot give any spiritual education, and may even be hostile toward your child's expression of faith
- Secular accreditation that most likely includes teachings of beliefs you may find opposite of your faith system (for instance, evolution, humanism, and multiculturalism)

- May devalue parental values or traditional family values
- May incorporate a tenure procedure that makes it difficult to fire a poor teacher
- Some may have larger class sizes, limiting personal attention
- Some schools may say they want parental involvement, but it can mean they want your money, not your opinion or input
- Peer values and influence may not be what you would want reinforced
- Budget expenditures may not be beneficial to your child
- Children of faith can become disillusioned, discouraged, and even depressed by the sinful behaviors, attitudes, and actions of those around them
- Classrooms may feel out of control (or actually be out of control) because the majority of students may not have been taught respect for authority, respect for others, and the teachers may or may not have backing for their classroom discipline policies

Private School/Christian School

Strengths
- Bible-based curriculum
- Christian teachers/role models who back up your beliefs
- Usually smaller class size
- Usually more personalized educational plans
- High opportunity for parental involvement
- Respect for authority encouraged

- Security and confidence builds as children see parents, teachers, pastors, and faculty all modeling the Christian faith
- Opportunity to come to faith in Christ as a result of what is learned in school
- Opportunity for children to see parents sacrificing for higher priorities
- Positive peer pressure
- Parents can work during school hours, and some schools might also offer quality after-school care options

Weaknesses
- You have to pay tuition while your tax dollars support the public schools
- Some have lower pay scales so they may not attract top educators
- Some may have strict background checks, educational standards, while others do not
- Students may develop an "us against the world" attitude or a fear of the "real world"
- Some parents may abdicate their role as spiritual mentors to the teachers with a "they get that at school" attitude
- A few students may develop a "been there, know that" attitude at church because they have been exposed to Christian teaching all week at school
- Some families might choose to work too hard to provide a Christian education, thus producing very limited family time due to two demanding careers
- There may not be programs or staff for special needs students

Private Non-Christian Schools

Note: Private non-Christian schools will have some of the advantages and disadvantages of both public and private Christian schools.

Strengths

- Smaller class sizes
- More personalized attention
- Parental involvement and quality control
- Opportunity to lead
- Opportunity to share Christ
- Tuition might provide more opportunities for arts, science, and technology
- Stronger discipline and class order

Weaknesses

- Some faculty with opposing beliefs
- Some students who may not hold your child's same beliefs or values
- Christian students might take flak for their faith or lack opportunity to express their faith
- Tuition
- Some might lack perks of larger institution

Homeschool

Strengths

- Many have parental co-ops, thus giving opportunities for personalized education in areas of specialties (music, science, art, technology, ministry)
- Very flexible on time, days, use of school hours, and learning methods
- Close interaction with adults, so less negative behaviors develop

- Individualized pace
- One-on-one or one-to-a-few allows for teacher (parent) to see any areas of weakness instantly
- Flexible schedule allows for different models of learning (perhaps traveling to the places you are learning about)
- Flexible schedule allows ample time for outside interests
- Good for families that live in remote areas (mission field, Christian camps, or far from any school)
- Flexible learning means student can explore areas of interest to them and not have to wait for the class or do busy work

Weaknesses
- Not enough social interaction on the peer level if the parent isn't careful to involve student in other outside opportunities
- "Been there, know that" attitude at church since they are exposed to a lot of Christian-based curriculum
- Expense of buying books, classroom supplies, and furnishings
- Home feels like school
- May be more difficult for parents to have two paychecks coming in
- May complete high school education very young and not be emotionally or socially ready for college

Questions to Ask When Considering School Choice
1. What are your top three priorities in choosing your child's education?
2. What are the lifestyle implications for each choice (for instance, mom would have to get a job to pay

tuition, mom would have to quit work to home-school, etc.)?

3. What are the areas you are most concerned about for your child's overall development?
4. What are your child's strengths? Which schooling option will reinforce those strengths and provide opportunities for future growth in those areas?
5. What are your child's weaknesses? What does each option offer to correct those weaknesses?

God loves your children even more than you do. As you prayerfully consider all your options, you can rest assured that He will lead you to make the right choices.

◆   ◆   ◆

A GRADUATION PRAYER

(A letter written to Brock Farrel from your mother when you were less than one, to be read upon your eighteenth birthday.)

I pray that by now you will have embraced and lived out your own faith in Jesus. I want you to have fallen in love with your Savior firsthand, not relying on Mom and Dad's faith, but on a strong faith of your own. I want you to know the joy of walking moment by moment in the power of the Holy Spirit. I want you to be able to discern God's will for yourself.

I want you to have a rich prayer life. I want your communion with God to be personal and real. I want you to have caught how we can use Scripture to pray, how to adore, confess to, and thank God, and supplicate on behalf of others and ourselves. I want prayer to be a one-on-one worship experience with the living God and you. I want you to really believe prayer works. By the time you are 18, I pray you will have influenced others to believe God for big things and have seen how a prayer movement can begin with just one—YOU! I want praise, music, and singing to come easily because your heart is rejoicing in the Lord's goodness. Sing—even if it is only a joyful noise unto the Lord!

I want you to have had and now enjoy great friendships. I desire for you the kind of true fellowship that can only happen when you choose to surround your heart with friends that love Jesus with all their hearts. I want you to have the courage and confidence to be a leader among your friends so they might draw nearer to Jesus because of you.

I want you to love God's Word. I want the Bible to daily be the lamp unto your feet and a light unto your path. I want you to know the thrill of walking in obedience to God—to find the gifts He's given you, to discern His will, to carve out your own ministry. I want you to have an eternal mindset and a worldwide vision for what God wants to do. He'll do some of it through you! No matter what your vocation, whether you are in full-time ministry or a secular career, living for Jesus is your first call. And if it is necessary to, I pray you'll have the courage of a Daniel, or a Joseph, and stand alone for your faith, your beliefs, and your convictions.

There will be some time when you will meet that special someone—so we want you to then leave us, your mom and dad, and cling to the one God has sent you! Make your love life a priority when you marry, and you will always have the passion of life the world so desperately seeks after. However, if God calls you to a single life for an extended period, let your passion be set on living a pure life, and God will fulfill your desires.

Children are a blessing from the Lord. I pray you'll be a terrific parent as you moment by moment ask God for wisdom to tenaciously love and raise those who will bear your name.

I pray you will gain an education so you can get the job God has for you. I pray you will save for the future, know the importance of tithing, and experience the pay-offs for being a self-motivated, hard worker. I pray you'll have a generous heart and share that which the Lord entrusts to you. I pray you'll be able to navigate the financial seas of credit, mortgages, checking accounts, and savings plans—all with the goal of being a good steward of all God has given. I pray you'll prepare well for the needs of your family in case of illness or death. I pray you will, above all else, keep a good name and good reputation.

I pray you will understand the huge price that was paid by this country's forefathers and be an involved citizen. My mother and my grandparents always reminded me that if I wasn't part of the solution then I was part of the problem. You know the solution to life's dilemmas—find a corner and make a difference! Be a leader. Be just and fair. Be a good friend and a fine neighbor. Treat others as God would treat you.

But please stop and smell the roses too. Let your heartstrings be moved by a beautiful painting, a great piece of literature, or a moving drama. Take a few moments each day to see God's beauty around you. You are a part of that beauty. Your body is God's temple. Take good care of it.

Don't forget the little things. Say please and thank you. Eat right. Laugh. Keep your accommodation neat enough to find what you need when you need it or to minister to a friend at a moment's notice. Keep gas in your car and money in your wallet. Don't presume upon your guardian angel and go knowingly into danger unless another's life depends upon it. Now that you are 18, you are an adult and many others depend on you.

There may come a time when my mind will fail, and my body will refuse to cooperate with my will. At that time, I may depend on you. My prayer is that you will be there for God, for your community, for your church, for yourself, for your spouse, your children, your grandchildren, and the host of friends you will gather. And I pray that as you someday stand over my grave, you will rise up and call me blessed because I prepared you, with all God's compassionate help and wisdom, for this day. You are no longer only my child. Over the years together, you have become my friend.

4

SHARE THE WEALTH

Developing Kids to Be
Learners and Leaders

Faith is a treasure passed from generation to generation. But in the midst of a hectic life, how does one make space for passing the baton? Jill Briscoe, an international speaker and writer, passed her faith to her daughter Judy. Then Judy became a mom, and wrote to me one day the following about passing the baton:

> When I was about to become a parent, my mom said to always remember that no matter what I was doing—laundry, cleaning, cooking, or helping with homework—the ground between my own two feet was holy ground. In other words, I should be ready at every moment to use the opportunities God would give me to influence whoever He placed in my path for Him. This is something I remind myself about frequently. Some of the chores related to mothering can

be mundane, and yet if I approach all of these tasks with the expectation that He can use even the most basic chore in His plan, then the chore isn't so mundane anymore.

I have three sons who are six, nine, and eleven. When my oldest son was almost four, he and my middle son and I were going to the grocery store. This was one of those mundane chores I didn't enjoy doing, especially because I had two little ones who would be asking for something in every aisle. As we drove to the store, my oldest son started asking some serious questions about heaven. By the time I pulled into the parking lot, he was saying that he wanted to invite Jesus into his heart. Before we got out of the car, Drew invited Jesus to be his Savior and Lord. This was a wonderful reminder to me that I needed to be ready and willing to use every opportunity to further His Word. The holy ground that day was the parking lot at the grocery store!

I too felt I was on holy ground as I thought about how to pass on my faith to my children. I looked at that list of traits and skills I had posted to remind me what I wanted to build into my two preschool boys. I had instituted a "quiet time" where I read to the boys, then put them down on their beds in each of their rooms. I then turned on a Christian music tape and left them with Bible storybooks (hoping they would nap!). I told them each day, "Every day, God wants us to have a quiet time, a few moments to read and listen to God through His Word. Mommy is having her quiet time in the kitchen. Now it is time for you to have fun with Jesus. Just remember, you need to stay on your bed. The toys are resting and God wants you to rest and spend time with Him. I'll see you in a few minutes." They usually made it through a book or two and perhaps one side of an audiotape before they drifted to dreamland. I held to my word too. I wanted to follow the example of Mary, Martha's sister. "Mary has chosen what is better, and it will not be taken away from her" (Luke 10:42). So, I tried to follow a pattern of delaying housework until after I had spent at least 30 minutes with God.

Discovering Key Traits

One day the list of traits I had written for my four-year-old, Brock, was again on my heart. *God, I have that little chore chart on the refrigerator, but that is just teaching Brock personal responsibility. What about all those other traits? How can I know that I have a plan that will work all the traits into his life by the time he is 18? It seems as if there is more I should do.* Then the Holy Spirit reminded me of a part of a talk I'd heard by Ken Poure, then the director of Hume Lake Christian Conference Center. All I remembered him saying was that every year, on each of their children's birthdays, he and his wife took that child out and wrote up a yearly contract that included new privileges and responsibilities.

I looked at my list of traits and skills. Which of these were really the most important? If I had to choose, which of these would I make certain happened?

Love God. That one for sure because most all the other character traits will develop if a person is connected to Jesus. After all, the fruit of the Spirit is love, joy, peace, patience, kindness, goodness, faithfulness, gentleness, and self-control—that was almost half the list of character qualities right there! Definitely *Love God.*

Lifelong learner. If I could get my kids to love learning, they would be motivated to learn most of the practical stuff and most of the relationship skills. Definitely a *Learner.*

What about the rest of the list? What's the common thread? Most leaders have these traits. *Leader*, yes! I've always believed that the most confident people are those who are on the offense, taking back ground, not on the defense huddled in a corner. I was raised to be a difference-maker. I want my children to be difference-makers too. But what if they are shy? What if they don't like the limelight?

Then God reminded me of the study of women of the Bible I had just completed. Those women (Deborah, Ruth, Esther) earned influence in a variety of ways. Some were quiet servants, and that's how their platform of influence was built. Yes, a leader, but in their own personality and leadership style. So the three main traits I decided we'd focus on were: *Love God, Learner*, and *Leader.* I thought, *Cool, 3 L's! That will be easy for my small sons to remember!*

Implementing the Traits

When Brock woke up from his nap, I tried it out on him. "Brock, you know what I want you to be when you grow up?"

"A policeman?"

"You can be anything you want—a policeman, a pilot, a pastor like Dad, or the president of the United States. But no matter what job you do, I want three things for you. I want you to *love God* with all your heart, soul, mind, and strength! I want you to always *love learning* no matter how old you get. And I want you to be a *leader.* I want you to lead your friends and not be a follower only. You can lead them using the talents, gifts, and strengths God will give you because there are all kinds of leaders. Brock, isn't it cool they all start with an—"

"L!" he shouted.

"That's right, an L. Love God, learner, and leader!"

All that day, as I saw these traits in Brock or his brother, I would comment and praise. I noticed Brock helping Zach pick up toys. "Brock, you are being such a leader! The best leaders are servants and helpers."

"Zach, you are looking at books. Books help us learn new things. You are a learner."

"Brock, will you bless our snack?" And after his short prayer, "Thanks for loving God. God loves it when we pray to Him."

I was so excited. I felt as though I finally had a simple enough framework to weave positive traits into my children in a natural, daily, moment-by-moment way. But I kept thinking about Ken Poure's tradition with his kids on their birthdays. Brock would be starting school the following fall. Wasn't there some back-to-school tradition I could do? I write goals for myself each August and January. I especially like doing this in August because that's when I set the pattern for my entire next year. Why couldn't I do this for and with my children each year?

I prayed over the idea for a while. Then one day I created a little chart with some pictures cut out from magazines that showed various chores. Brock couldn't read yet, but the pictures showed things I wanted him to take responsibility for: brush his teeth, make his bed, make lunch, feed the fish. At the top I wrote *Brock is a Learner and Leader who Loves God.* I listed all the character traits on the back of the chart and decided just to choose one to focus on that first year and wrote it on the front.

Then I thought, *Yuck, this just seems like work to me. What fun is a chart? If all I do is lay out work for my kids year after year, what is there to look forward to? At least Ken Poure took his kids out for lunch!*

Not just lunch—let's connect this to a special day! A Learner and Leader Day! We could do a fun family activity: bowling, movie, parks, maybe even Disneyland if we could ever afford it! Or maybe back-to-school shopping!

That's it! Every kid loves Christmas and birthdays because of the presents. We'll give presents on Learner and Leader Day. Something to help them either love God, learn, or lead! Or better yet, something that does all that and applauds the uniqueness, the calling we see God layering into their life! Yes! A celebration of God making them leaders! Cool. I can't wait until Bill gets home to run it by him!

When Bill got home from work, I could barely contain my excitement. I was hoping he'd be as excited as I was.

He was genuinely enthusiastic. "Honey, I think we should make it like a contract so the kids learn how business is run. And with the kids in youth group, those relationship and driving contracts seem to be good—at least for the families who are trying them out."

"Yes, a contract." I drew up a quick rough draft. "We could title it, 'Brock Is a Learner and Leader Who Loves God.' We'll list responsibilities on one side and privileges on the other. The leadership trait we are focusing on for this year will go on the top along with a verse for the year! They can memorize that verse to help them learn that trait. We'll choose it for now, but as soon as they are able, the boys can choose their own—ownership is good. Then we'll put the uniqueness we see God layering in them in a space at the bottom, and add the date and lines for signatures, like our mortgage! What do you think?"

"Sounds good so far," Bill said, smiling.

_____ Is a Learner and a Leader Who Loves God!

Privileges

Responsibilities

Responsibilities

Leadership Trait to Focus on this Year:

_____

Key Verse for the Year:

_____

Unique Treasure We See God Unfolding in You!:

_____

Signed_____(mom)

_____(dad)

_____(child)

Date: _____

"Oh, honey, what if when we present the gift, we do it with some kind of a blessing? You know, like in the Old Testament when Isaac blessed each of his sons. It was awesome the way he just spoke the truth over them."

"Definitely. We'll have to scale it back and make all this pretty simple while the boys are young, but I think this is definitely a plan that can grow with them."

The First Learner and Leader Day

The first August before Brock started kindergarten, we were pretty poor. We had moved to San Diego, still lived in an apartment, and funds were tight because Bill had actually taken a pay cut to take this senior pastor position. Not many churches were looking for 29-year-old senior pastors!

I had about $20 to work with. I bought a lunch box and Thermos at Pic-N-Sav for $3.99. Brock loved McDonald's Playland, so we could take him to lunch there, and he could play. I bought him a new T-shirt and a pair of pants on sale for a total of $9. If Bill and I had Happy Meals too, we could give the toys to Brock and he'd think he'd struck gold. I made up the Learner and Leader chart, wrote a verse with a permanent marker on the side of the lunch box, and added, "Brock is a Learner and Leader! Brock Loves God!"

We asked a friend to watch Zach so we could have one-on-one time with Brock and headed out the door to McDonald's. I explained the Learner and Leader tradition to Brock and then said, "Your dad and I have a gift for you. Each year we will give you a special gift to applaud the uniqueness, the calling, and the strength we see God layering into your life. Daddy has a special prayer he wants to pray over you first, then we'll give you the present."

Bill prayed, "Dear God, thank You for our firstborn son, Brock. He is getting so grown-up that he's headed off for kindergarten tomorrow. Thank You that Brock has a strong sense of righteousness. He wants people to follow the rules, and he speaks up and reminds people to do what is right. Bless him this year as he seeks to do what is right and follow a new set of rules that will come with starting school. Amen."

Then I handed Brock the wrapped lunch box. As he unwrapped it, he could see an astronaut on the side of the box. "Brock, you are going into unknown territory just like an astronaut. The sermon that Dad gave on his last day at Calvary Bible was called 'The Right Stuff,' and Daddy told the story of some brave astronauts who did what was right. They were brave and God brought them through.

"We see that same bravery in you. Last year, you spoke up and told someone that smoking would kill them. Last year, you made the junior high boy go down the slide the right way instead of climbing up the wrong way. You keep telling your little brother how to do things right—and sometimes you even remind Mom and Dad of the rules. We pray you will always have brave integrity and righteousness and that you will always want to speak up for what is right. This lunch box is our way of saying, 'Way to go!' "

Brock beamed. Bill and I looked at each other and smiled. We knew this Learner and Leader Day tradition was a keeper!

Creating a Plan for Your Own Learner and Leader Day

You can decide to do a Learner and Leader Day at whatever time of the year seems natural to your family. For example, you might like to connect it with your New Year's celebration when everyone is in a resolution-making mood. Or you might spread them out over the year, having one on each child's birthday (this option might be easier on the budget), or in September to celebrate "Back to School." One

woman I met at a Time Out for Moms conference has a
virtue of the month, and she focuses her entire family on
one character trait for that month. Every family is different,
so each Learner and Leader celebration will be tailored to
your family.

In our family we've also initiated a Summer Celebration,
a kind of mini Learner and Leader Day. My children are on a
traditional school schedule with summers off, so I want to
make good use of all that free time. For our Summer Celebration we all buy new bathing suits, restock our beach bag
with pool and beach toys, sunscreen, and new beach towels,
and then I lay out special summer goals for each son.

For example, one year I wanted the boys to understand
how the Bible came to them from the origin of Greek and
Hebrew. (We have a tradition that when each child can read
John 3:16 for themselves, they can choose their own new
Bible.) I wanted the learning to be more hands on and less
from a book, so we made scrolls and hid them and the rest
of the family tried to find them. Then I told the story of how
the Dead Sea Scrolls had been found by a shepherd boy in
some caves. We also studied how they were translated so
meticulously. We read about the lives of some of the great
leaders who had been martyred for trying to translate the
Bible into the common man's language and for printing
Bibles so every person could have them. We read the biographies of men like Tyndale and Wycliffe. We studied the
Reformation and Luther and nailed our own treatise to the
garage door.

One fun day, while studying the history of the Bible, I
told the boys about the Dark Ages, when even priests didn't
have Bibles and many church leaders couldn't even name
the 12 disciples. I told them it was a dark time in church history because pagan beliefs and human hunger for power

were mixed in with tradition. The truths found in the Bible were hidden away because so few people could read, let alone read a Bible. I explained that this then led to some ugly acts in church history, like the Crusades, where men in the name of Christ massacred and conquered to gain wealth and power for the Church. And I showed them pictures of the tools of the Inquisition and explained how true men and women of the Bible were often tortured and killed trying to get Bibles to families like ours.

Because so much of this happened in the Dark Ages, one day we made armor and newspaper swords and shields for each son. This led me to a passage in the psalms where God says He is our shield (Psalm 84:11). We looked up Bible-time shields and found that they were as tall as a man, covered with metal and leather, then decorated. They were three-sided so the only way a man could be hurt in battle was to step out from behind the shield, or to turn and run in retreat. Even the boys caught on to this word picture quickly.

"Mom, that means that if God is our shield, we'll only get hurt if we run away from Him."

"That's right."

"Or if we step out from behind the shield—like disobey, so we're out of His will."

"Right again. Everything that comes to us in life must first go through God and His loving character before it gets to us. That's why we are told to put on the armor of God in Ephesians. God's Word instructs us so we know how to stay behind God's shield of protection."

"That's why you want us to have a quiet time every day?"

"Right again."

We spent many days that summer reliving days from the Dark Ages. We read Arthurian legends. We read the biographies of Christian reformers. We studied castles and knights.

We watched movies with medieval themes. Then, at the end of the summer, we went to a medieval dinner theater where we ate food with no utensils and saw tools of the Inquisition and real knightly armor. The boys were amazed as they witnessed a reenactment of a knightly jousting competition.

That summer, I wanted my sons to come away valuing the Bible, but they gained much more. They gained a full appreciation of what honor meant. They discovered the horrible results that happen when God's Word is diluted and they were introduced to the ongoing battle between good and evil. They even enjoyed acting out excerpted scenes from Chaucer and Shakespeare!

Choosing a Learner and Leader Gift

I have a set of criteria in choosing the gift:

It must be *practical*, something I might have to buy anyway.

It must be *personal*. The child should be able to tell I thought about the gift.

It must be *prophetic*, meaning that it speaks the truth about the uniqueness, the calling, or the strength we see God building into each child.

Summers can be a terrific time to reinforce the values you want to develop in your child. If you are on a track system of schooling, then use the months off track for these more time-consuming projects. Here's some ideas to spark your own thinking:

- *Look Back.* Buy a set of books that describe what children are supposed to learn in each grade. Your public school office is supposed to have a "scope and sequence" available to parents. Most private schools or the curriculum publisher of the materials used should have something similar. Look over what they were supposed to have learned the past year and see where the missing pieces are and create a fun, hands-on learning project. Often these can be integrated into plans for the summer vacation.

- *Look Ahead.* Scan what is coming in the next year or two in their education and visit places, rent movies, read books, and give gifts that would expose them to that field of learning. They will feel great about themselves when the teacher gets to this place in the curriculum. You don't want to teach the exact same material or the child might be bored in class, but do expose them to the general field. For example, if my child will be making a solar system in school, I might take the family to an observatory. Or I might buy a telescope and do some stargazing or get those glow-in-the-dark star sets and let them build their own solar system on their ceiling so they can appreciate it every night at bedtime.

- *Look Deeper.* Apprenticeships and internships used to be the norm for preparing for productivity in the adult world. You can create opportunities for your child to be exposed to areas they might be interested in. Call a professional in that field and ask if you and your child might shadow them for a day. If the child is an older, responsible teen, you wouldn't need to go, but you don't want to give the appearance that the professional would be "baby-sitting." Offer to help the pro succeed. Be a part of a road crew, offer to work a day for free, or help them with a special event or major project. Encourage your child to go to the people at the top if they want to be a person at the top when older. Set up some adventures that will impact your child's future.

◆ *Look for Adventure*. Have your children brainstorm the first day of summer vacation all the wildest places, people, and things they'd like to go, meet, and try. Then prioritize the list and plan in Fabulous Fridays—a reward adventure for working hard all week. Feel free to add your ideas to the mix. Many cities have parenting magazines that list all kinds of learning adventures from drama and computer camps to visiting a llama ranch or the opera!

◆ *Look for Enterprise*. When my children have time off from school they always want to go, do, and spend! I look for ways to help them earn their own money to spend on their own interests. Mark, a man in our church, set up his son, Jesse, with his own plant business that runs just two weeks before Christmas. They go to a nursery and get whatever plants Jesse thinks will sell (a lot of poinsettias, of course). Then dad and son travel to all the businesses in the community to sell their wares. This is the money they spend on Christmas gifts. Some families use the holiday season for craft shows, others use summers for lawn mowing or lemonade sales. As a child, my summers were spent on 4-H projects from livestock to home decorating. I got to keep my ribbon money from the fair to buy something I wanted to learn more about. Also, my animals were sold and that money helped me get through college!

You don't have to call your celebration day Learner and Leader Day. You can make up your own name, like "Back-to-School Bonanza" or "Goal-Setting Getaway" or the "Smith Summer Send-Off." The only things you really need are the components of a Learner and Leader Day: (1) responsibilities for the coming year, (2) new privileges, (3) a leadership trait to focus on, and (4) a gift and blessing to applaud God's strength and calling in a child's life.

Praying for the Traits

Choosing the leadership trait to focus on for the upcoming year is probably one of the most important components of the Learner and Leader principle. Each year, Bill and I pray most of the summer and ask God to show us an area of weakness or incomplete character aspect in each of our sons.

For example, we have one son who was very, very shy. He wouldn't even ask for catsup at a fast food restaurant. Most of the time we had to order for him because the clerk couldn't hear him. He would regularly ask his brothers, "Tell them..." or "Can you go ask for me?" We knew we had to help him find his spine! One year we chose "initiative" as his trait, and we applauded him anytime we saw him do anything on his own. He received a standing ovation from our family the first day he went back to the counter and asked for catsup!

Another of our sons was pretty rough around the edges. He was a real jock and not very verbal. He made noises rather than used words to get what he wanted. He had more grunts, groans, and squeals than the average boy did. On top of that, he thought bodily functions and the noises they made were entertainment. He burped regularly at the dinner table, used his sleeve and underside of his T-shirt as a napkin, and wiped his nose on his T-shirt shoulder or one of his brother's shirts just to hear them scream. I remember thinking, *This kid will never get married! He's going to live with me the rest of his grunting and burping life!* That year we chose "being a gentleman" as his leadership trait. I taught him manners, or shall I say, *re*taught him over and over again. We ate off china and crystal and used linen napkins more that year than any before or since. We often ate by candlelight because I found he liked to light the candles and would sit more quietly at a table lit by candlelight.

That year when the science fair rolled around, we brainstormed ideas of what the kids could do their projects on. Zach, my rough-around-the-edges, gentleman-in-training, said, "Mom, I know you hate it when I burp. What if I do a project about what makes me burp?"

"I'm all for this idea, but I'm not sure how you'd run a scientific test to show how and why people burp. Let's go to the library and see what's there."

When we went to the library, I ran across an experiment book that showed how to measure the amount of gas in a soda. I showed it to Zach.

"Cool. I can use this to test different kinds of soda to see how much gas they have. Mom, I promise I will never again drink the soda that has the most gas!"

So we ran a test using different sodas in baby bottles and balloons and the results were that the darker the soda, the more gas—so cola was out! Zach was so proud of that experiment. He won the first place ribbon and science set for his class. And when the winner for the entire school was announced—it was Zach!

In my mind I remember sighing with relief and thinking, *Maybe there's hope.*

A few weeks later, a friend called me to report what had just happened at a birthday party she had given for her daughter. Seems Brock and Zach had sat down to eat pizza when Zach looked around and noticed that there weren't enough spaces for the moms at the party to sit down.

He elbowed his older brother in the ribs and said, "We should get up and give the moms our seats. That's what a gentleman would do."

Passing the Traits

One of my favorite families is that of my sister-in-law. I have been friends with her parents, Bill and Janeen Ezell, and then with Erin, before she married my brother. I have seen firsthand how well they live out their faith. Janeen is also known as one of the best Bible communicators in her region, and Erin is one of the best drama producers and directors in any church in the country (maybe I am a bit biased!). Now my nieces are carrying on the tradition of creatively sharing the message of the faith. I began this chapter with a story about passing the baton. Let's end it with another family's race. (Rebekah, the youngest little woman in this race, is just 13 years old.)

> As a child, even one raised in a non-Christian home, I (Janeen) somehow believed that Jesus was God. It wasn't until I was grown with two children of my own that I came to learn about the person and position within the Godhead called the Holy Spirit. That it is He who connects us with God in a personal way, and who also guides, counsels, comforts, and

teaches me everything about Jesus and His will for my life. When my children accepted Christ at an early age, I expected and taught my children that they would have the very same Holy Spirit living in them...not a miniature or child-size version, but the very same Spirit that filled Paul, Peter, and every believer. I expected that if they asked God in prayer, they would receive and experience the very same guidance, wisdom, and comfort as myself—I expected, and God did not disappoint them or me.

For as long as I (Erin) can remember, the only thing I ever wanted to do was be a great mom just like my mom. She was energetic, smart, beautiful, and fun. She loved God and knew Him unlike anyone else I ever met. I thought that the greatest thing I could ever be was to be like her. Even in high school, as my friends were pursuing college and careers, I prayed for a Christian man to love me and allow me to be his wife and a mother. I attended college and entered a career with a major oil company, but my hopes remained the same. When I was 20 years old, my dreams became a reality. I met and married a wonderful Christian man who loved me, and four years later I became a mom.

Now, as the mother of three children, I understand more deeply the incredible woman God gave to me as my mother. The courage she had demonstrated in trusting God for myself and my brother was so apparent when I became a parent myself and sent my precious child off to school for the first time. Her devotion is still so remarkable to me. I now sit by my children when a fever or flu ravages their little bodies, and I remember the many times Mom was there for me. Her understanding of God's Word and the time it took her to study, read, and pray challenge me today as I struggle to fit all my responsibilities into each 24 hours. I count it the greatest blessing of my life to have a mother who loved me, who cared for me, and who diligently taught me the joy in knowing and understanding God's Word. It is still today my greatest inheritance. It is still my highest aspiration—to be just like my mom.

The thing I (Rebekah) have seen in my Nana is the ability to communicate God's Word to other people so they can comprehend it and understand the promises God has for us. I also see that she is a loving, caring, and compassionate mother and Nana. These are the qualities I admire in her, and I hope that she will always stay that way.

What I see in my mom is a great, God-given talent. She can take music, scripts, sound, and lights and make them all into a presentation of God's Word. Through her direction, we can tell the story of Jesus' birth, life, death, and resurrection. I also admire her perseverance and imagination. She is loving and caring too.

Because of them, I do not want to be a person that is all show and no tell. I want to have depth. I want to be able to communicate God's promises to everybody. I want to be able to present it in an imaginative and creative way. I also believe that God will change me and mold me to have the amazing attributes of my mother and Nana.

These three women demonstrate how God can lead, guide, and carry faith from one generation to another, then another, then another. How will you choose to pass the baton on to your children?

Motivational Tools

How can you get a child to "do" the responsibilities delegated to him or her? Here are a few ideas from moms who've been there:

+ *Magnet Motivator.* "In our home, each morning, I place my children's responsibility magnets on the left side of the refrigerator. When they wake, each child checks his or her magnets to see what they need to do before they can leave for school or go out to play. As they complete each task, they move the corresponding magnet to the right or 'finished' side of the refrigerator. The magnets are easy to make. For the nonreader, pictures, symbols, or simple drawings can give direction. If the child makes his or her own set of magnets, then more ownership is given so motivation will be higher to accomplish the goal of moving the magnets."

+ *Help Them Bloom.* Write responsibilities on Popsicle sticks and each day have each child choose one or more. This is great for routine tasks of setting the table, clearing dishes, washing dishes, etc. One mom made flowers to go on top of each Popsicle stick. This vase of "flowers" sits atop her dining room table as a daily reminder to keep the kids involved.

+ *Work for Hire.* Pay an allowance of $1 per week for each year old a child is as a reward for assigned work (starting at age 5). Here's the catch—they pay for all their own desires. To make it more businesslike, if you have to clean up after them or do their chores, charge them a "maid's" fee.

+ *The Big Payoff!* When my sons were small, I motivated them by moving marbles from the sad jar to the happy jar anytime they did anything that would make Mom, Dad, or God glad. If they got a certain amount by dinner, there would be a special treat after dinner—usually a special activity with Mom or Dad. Or it can be a treat relating to bedtime, like a flashlight to read under the covers. Tammy sings a song about the highlights of each of her children's days while scratching their backs. Michele asks her children questions to get them talking at the end of the day, "What did you do to make God smile today?" For ideas, get *Mom's Jar of Questions.*[1] Another version of this is Super Kid Tickets. Give tickets for positive reinforcement and allow them to save up tickets and redeem them just like they would at an amusement park. Tickets can be used to stretch out a child's attention span and raise their goals to larger ticket items so they learn delayed gratification, a trait which will help them soar through their teen years!

◆ *Make a Game of It.* I used games to motivate my boys, much like Maria who sets a timer and makes cleaning up a race! She makes mealtime fun by having each child pretend to be a person at a restaurant. One person is the waiter, another the hostess, and so on.

◆ *Date with Mom or Date with Dad.* Every child, no matter what their age, loves a parent's undivided attention. The key to making this a strategic motivator is to let the child choose what to do on the date. Have a budget that is enough to get their attention. If you are working on a big attitude or behavior change, the carrot needs to be big enough to keep him or her trying.

- *Freeze.* When motivating kids to "work it out" in their sibling rivalry, try freeze tag. When in conflict, my friend Tracy yells "Freeze!" and everyone has to stop exactly where they are. No one can move until the conflict is resolved. Joy brings everyone to the table and everyone shares what the issue is and what they would like to see happen to solve the issue. No one can eat till the issue is resolved! If Karen hears a negative comment, she stops the accuser and has them give out two compliments for every one negative put-down given.

- *Life Report Cards.* Lynn says, "My mom always said, 'Give people bouquets while they can enjoy them.'" One mom of a special needs son with a learning disability gives a Life Report Card when the school report cards come out. She gives him A's in areas he is strong in: kindness, Lego building, and sharing. Esther has created a more God-centered reward system. Her children each have a points chart where they not only earn points for good grades and completing chores, but they get points for expressing positive character qualities like respect, good manners, and sympathy.

- *Good Morning!* Jenny greets her children with this little song: "Good morning, God, this is Your day. I am Your child, teach me Your way." Use birthday mornings to build esteem. Shawn climbs under the covers with her birthday child and retells the story of his or her birth and her delight to have God's gift of wonderful them! My own mom woke us up on our sixteenth birthday with breakfast in bed at the time we were born.

◆ *Reward Growth with Opportunities for Growth*. Nancy, whose son is now a divinity professor at Harvard, rewarded her children's Bible memorization with family "mystery trips" to the zoo, a bookstore, or other fun learning site. She went out of her way to reward excellence with opportunities to learn in a more excellent setting: Christian camps, mission trips, and teaching younger students. It is no wonder that when her son went to Wheaton to college and was looking for a mentor he walked into the president's office and asked the president himself—who said "yes!"

◆ *You Can Do It!* Jaime's little girl was anxious about being left for the Sunday school hour, so her mom began to tell her, "I know you are going to have a wonderful time. I know you are not going to cry. I know you are going to be a good girl and that the teacher will tell me super things about what a good helper you will be." By telling her daughter the positives beforehand, her daughter began to look forward to Sunday school. Jodie's son was homeschooled until age 11. On the eve before he was to attend "real" school, as he called it, he was a little nervous. Jodie wrote down a few Scripture passages about God's presence and strength and tucked them into her son's shirt pocket. The next day, anytime he was anxious, he pulled out a card and read it. Years later, as a 21-year-old college student, he is still in the habit of tucking God's Word into his heart—not just his pocket.[2]

More Than You Might Think!
What Kids Can Do at What Ages

Ages 2-4
- Ask them to pray
- Send them to retrieve things you need
- Put away toys and books
- Set table
- Clear their own plate (use plastic ware)
- Brush teeth
- Wash hands

Ages 4-5
- Put away groceries
- Set and clear table
- Put clean silverware away
- Make bed
- Dust
- Fold towels
- Get own snacks (make a snack drawer they can reach)
- Get own cereal, donuts
- Make simple sandwiches
- Pick up room (mark and label with pictures to make it easier)

Ages 5-6
- Help plan meals, help at grocery stores putting things in the cart
- Begin cooking (microwave and simple baking from a children's cookbook)

- Separate laundry, mate socks, put away clothes
- Answer the phone
- Help with larger chores like washing car
- Help with planting or raking in the yard
- Carry in groceries

Ages 6-7
- Lay out clothes for school
- Water plants
- Handle own bath
- Write simple thank-you cards
- Cook easy meals
- Hang up clothes
- Rake, recycle, compost, take out trash
- Bring in wood for fireplace
- Clean bathroom
- Empty dishwasher
- Get self ready for bed
- Get the mail
- Call a friend
- Walk to next-door neighbor's
- Take care of own bikes, skates, balls, etc.
- Take care of simple pets (fish, cats, gerbils, etc.)

Ages 7-9
- Neighborhood errands (like in a cul-de-sac or on same side of the street)
- Short errands when accompanied by older friends or older siblings
- Sweep walks, hose patios
- Vacuum house and car

- Responsible for own lunch money, homework, sports equipment, and hobby pieces
- Mop floors
- Iron with supervision
- Help with younger siblings
- Tithe
- Fold clothes
- Almost any household chore if trained and supervised
- Begin quiet time with Jesus
- Strip and remake bed
- Learn to sew and mend
- Clean blinds
- Help with campfire, bbq
- Paint with supervision
- Organize closets, own room, drawers
- Go places and return at specific times (get your child a watch)
- Help in ministry (greeter, help with younger children, pass out flyers, etc.)

Ages 10-11
- Clean refrigerator
- Learn how to use washer, dryer, dishwasher
- Wait on guests
- Be responsible for own hygiene
- Plan parties

Junior High
- Local errands on bike (in safe neighborhood)
- Responsible for own appointments, own calendar

- Stay alone and baby-sit
- Decorate room
- Learn adult crafts
- Social etiquette and boy/girl relations

High School
- At the high school level, teens should be seen as adults in training. As they enter high school, sit down and plan out how you will systematically give control of their life to them.

5

DIAMONDS
IN THE ROUGH

*Developing a Map
to the Hidden Treasure*

Humility is a virtue in God's eyes. John Wilmot, the Earl of Rochester once said, "Before I was married I had three theories about raising children. Now I have three children and no theories." Author Phil Callaway sums up the way many parents feel with the title of his book *I Used to Have Answers, Now I Have Kids*.

I think most parents have been there: the end of the rope, the place where you are at a loss for what to do and what to say. You've lost your patience, you've lost your way, and you might feel as if you've lost your mind. I'm convinced God sends strong-willed treasures to us so we don't fall into the trap of thinking we are the perfect parent, that we have all the answers. God wants to remind us that He is the only one who has the answers.

My strong-willed treasure is son number two, Zachery Johnathan Farrel. I should have clued in about the time when he was just walking. We were at a church afterglow (that delightful event where 500 men, women, and children crowd into a church fellowship hall to eat cookies and drink red punch). Zach was playing quietly with toys at my feet, pretending to be a compliant child. I was engaged in some deep girl talk when suddenly one of the students from the youth group came running up to me.

"Pam, do you know where Zachery is?"

I looked down at the floor. He was not there. I looked around, scanning the feet of the crowd. Then I began to panic.

"I do. He's over there, eating someone's Bible."

I ran across the gym, shooting up a prayer. "Lord, let it be someone who can handle it!"

None of this should have surprised me. Zach put everything in his mouth. I had Poison Control on speed dial.

I spotted him in a corner, blissfully gnawing on the corner of a beautiful new black Bible. I picked him up, pulled the piece of Bible out of his mouth, and tucked it in my pocket. Then I looked to see whose Bible he had eaten for dinner.

It was our associate pastor's. Whew! I ran across the gym to find him.

"Doug, Doug. I am so so sorry. Zach, he, um, he ate a page from your Bible."

Good-hearted Doug just laughed and in his sweet Southern drawl said, "Augh, just watch. It's probably 1 Corinthians chapter 13, and I'm just gunna have to love your kid!"

I pulled the crumpled piece of Bible out—and 1 Corinthians 13 was on one side of the page.

Before each of our sons were born, Bill and I chose their name and created a plaque with its meaning and a verse that captured that meaning. This is Zach's:

Zachery

The Lord Has Remembered
Jeremiah 15:15,16 (NASB)

Thou who knowest, O LORD, remember me, take notice of me, and take vengeance for me on my persecutors. Do not, in view of Thy patience, take me away; know that for Thy sake I endure reproach. *Thy words were found and I ate them,* and Thy words became for me a joy and the delight of my heart; for I have been called by Thy name, O LORD God of hosts" (emphasis added).

Zach had already lived up to his name verse!

The Beginning of the Treasure Hunt

When Zach was barely able to walk, he ran. And he ran everywhere. At the park one day while I was unloading Brock from his toddler seat, Zach unhooked himself from his seat, opened the car door, and ran straight for a 30-foot sculpture in the center of the park plaza and shimmied straight to the top before I could even catch up to him.

When we began building our house in San Marcos, Brock was a little over five and Zach a little over three. Zach and Brock were both given little carpenter's belts and plastic tool sets, but Zach was always replacing his plastic toys with the real thing. He actually was a very good helper. He would hold one end of the siding up and hammer in nails as well as many adults who came to help. Zach loved a challenge.

One day Bill was working on the framing of the house and I had an errand to run. Brock and Zach wanted to stay and play on our new property, and Dad promised to look after them. Before Bill knew it, Zach had climbed up a 30-foot eucalyptus tree (these trees are like tall twigs, straight and not very strong but very flexible. To a kid it would be like climbing a ticking metronome). Zach said his famous line, "Hey, look at me!" Bill looked to see his son up in the tree, higher up than our two-story home. Zach had his arms and legs wrapped around the thin tree trunk, and he was making the tree sway back and forth. Bill knew if he panicked, Zach could let go and fall three stories to the ground. But if he did nothing, Zach could get that tree swaying so much it would break in two and he would come hurtling down. So Bill coolly said, "Yeah, uh-huh, that's good, Zach. Can you come help Daddy?" Our little monkey simply shimmied back down the tree.

We've always said Zach marches to the beat of a different accordion. He was exceptionally agile, always landing like a cat on his feet. But he was also exceptionally nonverbal. He preferred making noises over making words or sentences. And he was strong-willed, all right. He, the senior pastor's son, and the youth pastor's son stole change out of the offering one Sunday when they were not quite four. They were headed to the church school kitchen to buy snacks when Bill caught them.

When Zach was about eight, almost nine, he had a medical problem that he couldn't control that added to his daily frustration with life. He had an older brother who threw up if he ever lied, so he rarely did. In fact, Brock got most of his rebellion out of his system before he was two, and it's been pretty much easy sailing with him. Then along came Caleb, and Zach, who was the darling baby, was bumped from his prima donna position in the family to that dreaded middle spot. Bill and I were sensitive to his plight, so we were careful to never compare the boys but rather to applaud each of their unique strengths.

Zach was a talented athlete. He taught himself how to ride a bike when at age three he found Brock had left his bike in the driveway. Zach simply jumped on it and rode away—first time, no wobbling, no falls, total confidence. He did that with rollerblading—down a hill the first time out on skates. He was also a courageous skateboarder and mountain biker. *No Fear* T-shirts were made for boys like my Zach.

And Zach was a good-looking kid. People often commented on his handsome appearance and his strong, fit body. His eyes danced and sparkled at the thought of a new adventure, a new challenge.

But when he was almost nine, life seemed to be sapping his tenacity. He began to lose ground in school. Homework each night became a battle. Progress was only made when I placed an M&M at the end of each row of math problems.

He became more and more sullen. He acted out with more and more explosive anger at his brothers. He hated anything new. Any change in the routine or plan sent him reeling into a tantrum. My brave, happy-go-lucky, adventurous son was turning inward, spiraling downward into a depression, drowning in a pain he was unable to articulate. I fought to keep his head above these emotionally turbulent waters.

One day he came into the house from playing outside with his brothers. Brock and Caleb were in tears. He was beating on them again. Zach stomped into the house, bumped one brother and socked the other right in front of me.

"Zach," I bent down and whispered intently into his face, "you cannot do this. Hitting is inappropriate. Go upstairs and I will come up to talk to you."

Zach stomped up the stairs, knocking his brothers over in the process. He slammed the door to his room and threw a baseball at it, knocking a hole in the door. He then picked up his favorite clay art piece he had made and smashed it into the wall, breaking it into little pieces. I bounded up the stairs just behind him. I prayed all the way up the stairs because I had made a commitment to never, ever discipline in anger. But I wasn't angry. I was scared, scared for my son.

I walked into the room, bent down so I was eye to eye with him and said firmly but calmly, in more of an intense whisper than a yell, "Zachery, this is inappropriate. I know you are angry. I know you are upset. But you cannot use your fists to show it. You have got to learn to use words to express your feelings."

Zach exploded and yelled back at me, hands on his hips, "You want words! You want words! Then I hate myself and I hate my life and if God made me, I hate Him too!"

I was filled with shocked silence. I simply replied in a whisper, "I'll be right back."

I ran to my room in tears. I threw myself across my bed and desperately prayed to God, "Lord, I am a pastor's wife who is raising a little atheist upstairs. I am so afraid for Zachery. I don't know what to do. I know he is angry at his medical condition. He might even be upset because it has made him gain some weight so he might not feel like himself. Maybe being in the middle is hard. I don't know. I don't know anything anymore. All I do know is that Psalm 139 says he is fearfully and wonderfully made. I believe that. I believe there is a gift You place in each and every one of us. But God, Zach is so angry he cannot see the treasure You have placed inside him. Help me help him see that treasure!"

Making a Treasure Map

Then the idea came. I ran to the office and pulled out a piece of poster board. I drew a treasure map on it and drew a bunch of lines and a treasure chest at one end, glued a quarter or two onto the map, and marched myself back upstairs where Zach stood, just as I had left him.

"Zach, here's the deal. You and I are going to go on an adventure. See, God has placed a treasure, a special uniqueness inside every person. There is a treasure in you, Zach," I said as I tapped on his chest. "You and I and God are going on a treasure hunt to discover that hidden treasure. So here's the plan. I am going to ask you everyday to name one thing positive about your day and one thing you think you did well. Then once a week, while everyone else is in second service at church, you and I are going on a breakfast date and we're going to talk about what we see God is showing you about the treasure inside you. We're going to do this for at least six weeks, maybe eight. At the end of that time, I am going to invest some money. I am going to invest that money in the treasure God has shown is in you. Zach, you are a special guy. We all love you, and God loves you most of all. Let's ask God to help us discover your treasure."

I prayed over him, then I asked him to pray and all that came out through sobs and tears was a faint, "Help me, God."

The next day after school, I got the Treasure Map down off the wall where I'd posted it. "Zach, what's one thing positive that happened today? Let's write it down."

Zach looked at his feet silently. "Come on, honey. Just one thing positive about your day." He kept staring at the ground as if a hand would appear and write the answer on the carpet in front of him. This response, actually nonresponsive attitude, had become familiar to me when dealing with him. I felt that the drawbridge was up and knew there were alligators in the moat. Zach had a chronic Eeyore-like attitude. Eeyore, in the Winnie-the-Pooh tales, always hung his head, moped, and said, "It's hopeless, it's never going to work." That was Zach, hopeless.

I spoke for him, "Honey, you are alive." (I was holding back my own frustration because I was sarcastically thinking, *Yep, you are alive—because I haven't killed you from sheer frustration, kid!*) But God miraculously replaced my frustration with compassion, and I wrapped my arms around that sullen, stiff little body and whispered excitedly into Zach's ear, "Zach, you're alive! You're alive. I am so glad God gave you to me! You're mama's special treasure!" And I took the pen and wrote on the poster: *Zach is alive.*

The next day, right after school, Zach ran upstairs and brought the Treasure Map to me. He had several answers to the two questions: *What was positive about your day? What is something you think you did well?*

Soon, there weren't enough lines to hold all the positive things Zach was seeing around him. Each week, he couldn't wait for our mom-son date. And every week, I learned more and more about him. Because he still struggled with finding the words to express himself, I took out a magnet that had faces that expressed different emotions. The magnet had a little square on it that said, "Today I feel" and you can move it to faces that express emotions: exhausted, confused, ecstatic, guilty, suspicious, angry, hysterical, overwhelmed, frightened, and a host of others ranging from excited to depressed. I taught Zach the meaning of each word, sometimes acting out how the feeling looks and how people act if they are feeling that way. I read and read and read everything I could find about children and their feelings. I adapted every learning activity I had ever heard about or used in any setting to try to teach Zach how to understand and express verbally what was going on inside his head.

Sometimes he became frustrated because he couldn't find the words to use to help me understand him. At those moments, often as he was screaming or thrashing about in anger, I would simply wrap my arms around him and hold him ever so tightly, and whisper, "I love you, Zach. Nothing can make me not love you. You can never push me away. I'm here to stay. You and I and God will figure this out. Nothing's too tough for God. Nothing's too tough that my love and God's wisdom can't handle. I'm here, baby. I'm here. I'm here." I found that when I reacted with stubborn love, he felt more secure and safe, and then he was able to think better and slowly he would try something new or a new word or way of expressing himself.

Week after week, I felt like I was tapping into the real Zach, the Zach God had created. Zach and I were beginning to see his treasure.

At the end of those eight weeks, I had discovered a lot about my son. I had always known he loved sports, particularly biking and baseball, but what I hadn't realized was that Zach loved those things because he loved the camaraderie of the experience. I knew Zach had many friends (which actually stumped Bill and me because we wondered how a kid who didn't speak much at all could make friends). Zach loved people. People gave him energy. Being with people motivated him. Bill and I began to see a pattern. Zach was often stubborn, fearing new things, but we could always convince him to try something new if we appealed to his sense of loyalty to a person. We found the people in his life who expressed to Zach how much his contribution would mean to them personally would get the most out of him.

We also discovered he loved music. And we saw another repeating pattern on the map. Zach loved to set and reach goals. We learned so much about our son in just two months' time by following our Treasure Map. It was fun and exciting for all of us.

With the money I had set aside, I bought some baseball equipment. I bought some tickets to a Christian concert for Zach and some of his buddies. We did the Treasure Map from Christmastime until about Zach's birthday at the end of February, then baseball season started. Zach made the all-star team. At the end of the season, the coach brought Zach up in front of his teammates and all the parents and said about my strong-willed treasure, "Zach has the best attitude of any kid I have ever coached."

I wanted to joyfully proclaim, "You don't know how far he's come! Praise God!"

Dad's the Difference

While I was helping Zach discover the treasure inside, Bill was teaming up to convince Zach God's plan was best. On those days when Zach was in his Eeyore mood, sitting and declaring for the umpteenth time, "I can't do this. I'm so stupid," Bill would sit with him.

We have seen in our 20 plus years of ministry that the stronger willed the child is, the stronger dad needs to be. When we say dad is stronger, we don't mean more physically aggressive or verbally abusive—far from it. Rather dad needs to be tenaciously diligent to speak the truth in love and back up every discipline plan and not cave in.

For example, when Zach would say, "I'm stupid" and refuse to do his homework, Bill would simply say, "You are not stupid. Do not say you are stupid. Zach, you can have a good attitude or a bad attitude, but either way, you are doing this." Or Bill might say, "You can make this hard on yourself, or easy on yourself, but you are doing this." Once when one of Zach's pouting tirades had extended for hours, I heard Bill quietly but firmly tell Zach, "Son, I will outlast you." And that is the key, dad and mom becoming a united team, backing each other up, relieving one another when their own feelings become frustrated so they can outlast the strong-willed child. (Suggestions to single parents: The single moms in our church who handle their children best have banded together to have a support net so that if they are exhausted and need backup, they can call one another.)

However, dad plays a strategic role. The earlier a child knows that dad means business and dad will always keep his word, the better for the strong-willed child. These kids are looking for boundaries, and they want to know you can be depended on. They respect commitment even when they don't like it. Bill invests time in Zach too with father-son trips, coaching his basketball teams, and helping him with special school projects.

Bill and I often prayed together for Zach and with Zach that God would lead him out of the quicksand of negativity and onto the solid ground of the truth. Bill was tenacious in reminding Zach, "We don't want you to be like your older brother. We don't expect that and neither does God. We want you to be Zach. Just be the best Zach you can be."

Bill spent hours building skateboard ramps with Zach, taking him to skate stores and competitions and scanning photos of him skateboarding into the computer so Zach could create posters, clothing decals, and other high-tech identity icons. He wisely saw that skateboarding was one way for Zach to do something excellent in an area Brock wasn't good in. It all worked. And it was WORK. But when you are battling for the life of your child, no sacrifice is too high.

Going the Distance

There is a story in 1 Kings that tells of a woman who was willing to risk on behalf of her son. Elijah was a prophet of God, and God had a plan for providing for Elijah's need and for the widow and her son—but they didn't know it—yet. God told Elijah:

> "Go at once to Zarephath of Sidon and stay there. I have commanded a widow in that place to supply you with food." So he went to Zarephath. When he came to the town gate, a widow was there gathering sticks. He called to her and asked, "Would you bring me a little water in a jar so I may have a drink?" As she was going to get it, he called, "And bring me, please, a piece of bread."
>
> "As surely as the LORD your God lives," she replied, "I don't have any bread—only a handful of flour in a jar and a little oil in a jug. I am gathering a few sticks to take home and make a meal for myself and my son, that we may eat it—and die."

Elijah said to her, "Don't be afraid. Go home and do as you have said. But first make a small cake of bread for me from what you have and bring it to me, and then make something for yourself and your son. For this is what the LORD, the God of Israel, says: 'The jar of flour will not be used up and the jug of oil will not run dry until the day the LORD gives rain on the land.' "

She went away and did as Elijah had told her. So there was food every day for Elijah and for the woman and her family. For the jar of flour was not used up and the jug of oil did not run dry, in keeping with the word of the LORD spoken by Elijah (1 Kings 17:9-16).

Look Back

What has God already done for you? He gave you this child, He gave you His Word that explains that God created this child, He knows every hair on his or her head, and He has provided to keep you and your child alive. God even gives reminders in His Word, that "with man this is impossible, but with God all things are possible" (Matthew 19:26), "nothing is impossible with God" (Luke 1:37), and God can do "exceeding abundantly beyond all that we ask or think" (Ephesians 3:20 NASB). Look back, thank God for your child, and thank Him for every provision or bit of wisdom He has already given. As you look back, your faith will be built up for the future.

I keep quiet time journals and prayer notebooks where I record my requests. When times get tough with my children, I reread those journals and notebooks. I also pull out our photo albums. Sometimes seeing reminders of God's faithfulness in the past gives me the faith to step forward and deal with the present.

Get the Best Help Possible

When a tough time comes for your child, don't waste time worrying—go directly to the top. Go to God and ask Him for a solution. Go to the best Christian leaders in the field, go to the best doctors. Now is not the time to worry about hurting someone's feelings. When a child is drowning, you don't take an opinion poll on the beach to see who the crowd feels is the best rescuer. Instead you run to get the lifeguard, a person trained to rescue—an expert.

That's what the widow did:

> Some time later the son of the woman who owned the house became ill. He grew worse and worse, and finally stopped breathing. She said to Elijah, "What do you have against me, man of God? Did you come to remind me of my sin and kill my son?"
>
> "Give me your son," Elijah replied. He took him from her arms, carried him to the upper room where he was staying, and laid him on his bed. Then he cried out to the LORD, "O LORD my God, have you brought tragedy also upon this widow I am staying with, by causing her son to die?" Then he stretched himself out on the boy three times and cried to the LORD, "O LORD my God, let this boy's life return to him!"
>
> The LORD heard Elijah's cry, and the boy's life returned to him, and he lived. Elijah picked up the child and carried him down from the room into the house. He gave him to his mother and said, "Look, your son is alive!" (1 Kings 17:17-23).

I believe parents should take this principle of going to the best one step further: Get the best advice and training *before* you need it. When I was still single, I went to the Institute of Biblical Studies held by Campus Crusade for

Christ. At age 19 I sat for weeks and listened to Dennis Rainey, now the president of *Family Life Today*, talk about marriage and family. When Bill and I were newlyweds, we watched all of the James Dobson videos on family even though we didn't have children yet. When we were expecting, we read and did the Bible study Norm Wright had out then called *Preparing for Parenthood*. And we did a Bible study together called *Discipline Them, Love Them*.

Then when Brock was under a year old, I made it a habit to listen to Focus on the Family radio daily, and I have added to that programs like *Family Life Today, Parent Talk, The Family Workshop, Crown Financial Concepts*, and other family programming. I have subscribed to all kinds of parenting magazines, and before Brock was a year old, I had read over 100 books on parenting. I figure if I get one good idea from a book, it is worth the money I paid for it (but most were available in my local library and some churches have libraries as well).

When my two oldest were just toddlers, I hung out with several older women who were leaders in Bible Study Fellowship and watched how they parented. I asked Nora, a woman who had four terrific kids, two in our youth group and two in full-time Christian service, to be my mentor mom and share with me how she parented. I had a wonderful mother, but I came to Christ before my mom and we grew in Jesus together. My parents also had a turbulent marriage due to my dad's alcoholism, so I didn't see modeled a mom and dad who both loved God and loved each other during my developmental years. I gleaned from my own mother all the wonderful creative ways she mothered me, and I know my tenacious love comes from her example, but I wanted more information for my own family.

I also made careful observation of the families in the youth group we pastored. I noted how the best kids in the youth group were parented—and I even started a list in one of my quiet time journals called, "Things I will never do when I have teenagers: Hills NOT to die on."

On that list were things like:

- Do not freak out if my 15-year-old daughter wants her own phone. If she wants to pay for a second line and the monthly bill, let her.
- Do not ground my kids from youth group. Find another way to punish them, preferably working them hard and limiting TV, social activities, and other things not related to God.
- Care less about the length of their hair and more about the condition of their heart.
- Do not make my kids be a certain way simply because I think it makes me look good.
- Do not live through my child. Have my own life, have my own dreams and goals, and let them have their own dreams too. My dream for them may not be their dream. Be more concerned that they find God's dream for their life, not live out one I might have for them.
- Do not be legalistic. Major on the majors.

By having all this information swimming around in my head, when Zach hit his tough spot, I knew God would have an answer. I knew to pray, plan, and not just react out of fear, frustration, or anger. I had a host of positive reinforcement ideas already in my head, and I had example after example from real life and from the Bible of what tough love and committed love looked like. By preparing and informing yourself ahead of time, you are less likely to make a mistake that will make matters worse.

Patient Parenting Produces a Prize

Today, I have a new son. Zach's nickname around our church is "Pastor to Preschoolers" because he works in children's ministry, and he knows the name and about every kid in the department. They follow him like the Pied Piper around church. Zach has excelled in skateboarding, and he is in guitar lessons because music is just one more avenue he can express himself in. However, by far, Zach's strength is in helping people. He is a sensitive motivator and a great friend. He is the most attuned to my emotions. He'll often notice if I have a headache or if I seem preoccupied or stressed. Zach, as a 14-year-old football player, always kissed me goodbye when I dropped him off at practice. He is never too proud to express his feelings about people. He has a fun sense of humor, and he loves to make people laugh.

This year, as a freshman at public high school, Zach went out for football. He started out third string, a far cry from his older brother, the starting varsity quarterback. But being the star isn't what is important to Zach. People are.

Zach held a pizza party for his teammates, and at it he shared his personal testimony, which included a piece of his story, "Guys, God gives me the strength every day to face my fears. Right now, God is giving me the courage to talk to you. God can give you that same strength and courage if you ask Him." That day 16 of his teammates prayed to receive Christ. His coach has affectionately nicknamed him "The Preacher" because of his positive impact on the team. At the freshman football dinner, his friends saved him a spot and wouldn't start eating until Zach came in and selected someone to pray over the meal.

Because he feels great about who God made him, he is able to make others feel great too. Of my children, currently Zach is the most serious about praying about going into ministry. He is researching Christian counseling, youth ministry, and Christian camp ministry.

This year, I spoke at a Time Out for Moms conference, and I asked my sons to make a video giving advice to moms. This is what Zach said, "There was a time when I felt stuck in my life. I didn't like myself much, and I felt like a failure. But my mom never gave up hope in me. My advice is to never give up on your kid, no matter how hard it gets. My parents never gave up. My mom helped me realize I had a treasure, a uniqueness, and that God made me special for His purpose. Your kid has a treasure too. Don't give up...go on a treasure hunt instead."

God's Treasure in You!

Follow the map to find your treasure.

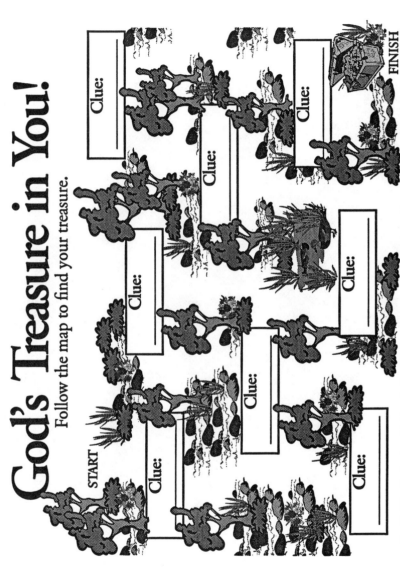

START

Clue:

Clue:

Clue:

Clue:

Clue:

Clue:

Clue:

Clue:

FINISH

6

HELPING YOUR CHILD STAKE THEIR CLAIM

Mapping Out the Uniqueness of Your Child

When archaeologists are looking for treasures from past civilizations, they stake out an area, mark off plots, meticulously number them, and record every bit of information they find as they painstakingly chip, chisel, whisk, and sweep bits of earth away. These scientists are masters of observation. They know the smallest clues, when pieced together, can lead to the greatest of finds.

In the same way, as we use resources to unearth clues that lie beneath the surface of our child's soul, we can parent more personally by adapting to meet the need of the child. We can also guide more confidently, because it isn't just our wisdom, but the wisdom of specialists we have available. I will share many resources that have helped me over the years see my own children more clearly—the positive and the negative! Each resource I share is a wealth of information all on its own. I will give only a snapshot, a bite-size piece of these helpful tools. I encourage you to buy the books and resources and make further investigation using each resource to piece together a beautiful mosaic of each of your children.

Understanding the Gender Difference

In our book for married couples *Men Are like Waffles— Women Are like Spaghetti*, Bill and I explore the differences in the genders. There is an entire chapter devoted to parenting boys and girls. In a nutshell, men are like waffles: Men process life in boxes. If you look down at a waffle, you see a collection of boxes separated by walls. The boxes are all separate from each other and make convenient holding places. That is typically how a man processes life. Their thinking is divided up into boxes that have room for one issue and one issue only. The first issue of life goes in the first box, the second goes in the second box, and so on. The typical man then spends time in one box at a time. Social scientists call this "compartmentalizing"—that is, putting life and responsibilities into different compartments. As a result of thinking through life in boxes, men are by nature problem solvers.

Women are like spaghetti. In contrast to men's wafflelike approach, women process life more like a plate of spaghetti. If you look at a plate of spaghetti, you notice that there are individual noodles that all touch one another. If you attempted to follow one noodle around the plate, you would intersect a lot of other noodles, and you might even switch to another noodle seamlessly. That is how women face life. Every thought and issue is connected to every other thought and issue in some way. Life is much more of a process for women than it is for men. This is why women are typically better at multitasking.

There are key parenting principles to keep in mind for each gender. For example, Bill says that boys are the people of the ladder and girls are the people of the circle. This means that one-upmanship is a necessary and expected behavior in a boy. He wants to be the "best" at something, and he'll risk interpersonal conflict to attain it. By helping a son achieve and feel confident in an area, you will find he can become a better sport if he does experience loss. Keep in mind that a boy will strategically organize his life in boxes and then spend most of his time in the boxes he can succeed in. Boys can become too singular in focus, ignoring areas in which they feel less competent, so parents are wise to work extra hard to help their sons experience successes in areas that are vital for life—say reading and math.

When men perform as well as they expected at a particular task, they tend to attribute their success to their own skill or intelligence. If they perform below their expectations, they tend to blame it on bad luck or some factor that is out of their control.[1] This habit of blaming others can be curbed if a parent teaches a son to own up to failure and take responsibility for mistakes.

On the other hand, women tend to underestimate their abilities, and when they perform only to the level of their low expectations, they tend to attribute it to their lack of ability or intelligence. But when a girl exceeds her low prediction for achievement, she tends to attribute it to good luck or some other factor beyond her control.[2] A wise parent will compliment her when she recognizes that her own hard work paid off. Women tend to lead by consensus, which can be a great people skill, but it could also hold them back if they have to take a vote on every issue that needs a decision!

Because my sons are like waffles, and they tackle one problem at a time, I have learned not to give a verbal to-do list like, "Go get your black sweats, put your shoes away, take out the trash, and feed the dog." Rather, I write out the list (a piece of paper is a great "box"). This skill will help young men to learn to multitask.

When stress hits, boys will want to go to their favorite easy boxes (places they feel successful or can unplug) and daughters will want to talk! Sons will feel more loved if they are given space to fish, to be on the computer, or do a hobby. A daughter will feel loved if she is listened to.

Understanding Varying Personalities

There are many great personality tools that can help you glean vital information into tapping into the primary motivator for each personality type. But let's start with some basics. On the chart on the opposite page, you see four quadrants. Those personality types to the left of the center line are primarily people-driven personalities. I am married to one. Bill is a pastor, but he has a difficult time staying on task. Not because he can't. He graduated seminary with honors. He was an architect major when I met him—but he didn't stay an architect because as he shared Christ and saw people's lives change, he knew he wanted to invest his life in people, not buildings. If he is working on a task, and a person walks by and they seem to be a little blue, Bill cannot ignore them to complete the task. People are his priority. That's what makes him a great shepherd—but it is also what keeps him from completing tasks in an efficient manner.

Zach has this same trait. If he has a choice between breaking down the set after church or baby-sitting the staff

PEOPLE ORIENTED	TASK ORIENTED	
PERSONALITY TYPE I POPULAR Sanguine  Motivated by: ATTENTION Brawner: Otter Phillips: Expressive Disc: Inspirational Littauer: Yellow like the sun Biblical Example: John the Baptist	**PERSONALITY TYPE II** POWERFUL Choleric Motivated by: Being in CONTROL Brawner: Lion Phillips: Driver Disc: Dominant Littauer: Red like fire Biblical Example: Peter	E X T R O V E R T
PERSONALITY TYPE III PEACEFUL Phlegmatic Motivated by: RESPECT & ACCEPTANCE Brawner: Retriever Phillips: Amiable Disc: Steady Littauer: Green like grass Biblical Example: Barnabus	**PERSONALITY TYPE IV** PERFECT Melancholy  Motivated by: ANSWERS & STRUCTURE Brawner: Beaver Phillips: Analytical Disc: Cautious Littauer: Blue like the ocean Biblical Example: Martha	I N T R O V E R T

kids, he'll entertain the kids in a heartbeat. If he has homework and friends over, he has learned that he has to create a homework club so he can get his homework done. He studies best over conversation and chips. Brock, on the other hand, would rather lock himself away in his own room to study because he says, "Studying in a group is a waste of time. You have to wait until everyone gets it, and half the time they aren't even talking about anything remotely related!"

You guessed it, he is task-oriented. The task-oriented personalities are the two on the right side of the chart. Now, it isn't that task-oriented people don't like socializing; they do. But if they have to choose between getting the job done and talking, they'll get the job done every time. If I want something done at home, I'll ask Brock and he'll have it done in an instant so he can go on to the tasks he enjoys most. Many people that are great with technology have this personality trait. Brock can do almost anything on the computer I need done, he can fix VCRs, set up sound systems, and build a set of bookshelves or a desk without even looking at the directions. He loves math. Life to Brock is one big equation. You put in the right variables, and you'll get the desired outcome every time.

But if you want counseling, don't ask Brock. His answer will always be the same. "You are having a problem with temptation. Then just don't do it anymore. Problem solved." If a person wants sympathy, Zach is a much better counselor. He'll sit down with a person, usually approaching them because he can read discouragement or depression in a person's face. He'll ask, "What's wrong?" He'll listen attentively, he'll pray, and he'll carry their pain with him. He always wants to take people places and buy them resources he thinks will help.

Introverts and Extroverts

Those personality types above the line are extroverts. Those below the line are introverts. Be careful, this doesn't mean one is loud and the other quiet. Extroverts feel more secure and at peace when all the ducks of their life are lined up. They tend to ask questions like: *Am I spending enough time with God? Am I balanced in my personal disciplines of prayer, Bible study, witnessing, fasting, and memorization? Am I spending enough time with my family? Am I spending enough time with my friends? Am I spending enough time at work to meet the goals I have set?* They are life organizers, and if they feel they have the right organizational plan, they are as happy as clams.

Introverts tend to ask questions like: *Do I feel connected to God? Is my personal prayer life deep, and am I sensitive to God's call and leading? Am I sensing a connection with those I love? Am I relating well to my friends? Is my work fulfilling? Do I have a sense of personal peace and tranquility?* When these people are emotionally connected and fulfilled, they are at peace.

There can be quiet extroverts. Zach is an extrovert. For years we couldn't figure out how someone who doesn't seem to talk could have so many friends! Bill is an outgoing, verbal introvert. He is a gifted communicator, entertaining, and practical, but he has an ability to go straight to the heart—which comes because the heart is a priority to him. Bill is miserable if he is not emotionally connected to those he cares about.

The Four Basic Temperaments

We'll look at the Greek names for the four temperaments and a few basic traits for each one. The original personality types were: Sanguine, Choleric, Melancholy, and Phlegmatic. In her book *Raising Christians—Not Just Children*, Florence Littauer uses some easy to remember terms:

Sanguine	POPULAR	is YELLOW like the sun
Choleric	POWERFUL	is RED like fire
Melancholy	PERFECT	is BLUE like the ocean
Phlegmatic	PEACEFUL	is GREEN like grass[3]

When taking a personality test as an adult, try to think back to what you were like as a child of seven or eight. Often, as adults, we have learned to mask our true loves in order to please other people or, in a positive way, we have gained the skills to round us out and strengthen our perceived weaknesses with a goal of becoming more like Jesus. (Jesus does, of course, have *all* the strength of all the personalities and *none* of the weaknesses.)

We have found that our children's personality types were easier to discern in the "tweenager" time of life from nine to thirteen. When Brock was about nine, we were teaching personalities at our church's family camp. We were using Jim and Suzette Brawner's book *Taming the Family Zoo,* which uses animals to describe the different personalities. The Choleric, a personality motivated by power, is a Lion; the fun-loving Sanguine is an Otter; the diligent Melancholy is a Beaver; and the amiable Phlegmatic is a Golden Retriever. When Brock took the test he came out even in two personalities, one being a Lion. I said, "Let me take the test for you, Brock. I'll answer how I see you." The results were an overwhelming Lion outcome. To which Brock replied, "I am not a Lion! Don't tell me I am a Lion. I will let you know what I am after I have decided!" (A *very* typical Lion response!)

One of the best places to receive training on the personalities is through Florence Littauer's CLASS seminars. One year a counselor named Sue attended. She worked in a home for underprivileged, abused, and orphaned children. Upon return to her job, she began to categorize the children into personality types. She gave them a simple survey and one of the questions was, "If you could be any kind of person in the world, what or who would you be?" Here are some to the answers she forwarded to Florence:

"The Populars wanted to be actors, comedians, TV stars in soap operas, cheerleaders, salesmen, Cinderella, or Miss Piggy.

"The Powerfuls wanted to be kings and queens, the president, Hitler, owners of big houses and limousines, highway patrolmen, and football players.

"The Perfects dreamed of being musicians, artist, poets, bankers, Mozart in *Amadeus,* and Garfield the Cat.

"The Peacefuls wanted to be rich so they didn't have to work, live on lakes with boats and canoes, be golf pros, and have long vacations and more recess."

As she worked with the groups she found the Populars were motivated by abundant praise, the Powerfuls by appreciation of all their achievements, the Perfects by her encouragement and observation of how well they had done each task, and the Peacefuls by a slow building of a trusting relationship where they were finally convinced she valued them.[4]

The Powerful

The traits of the powerful Choleric are: extrovert, task-oriented, a decision-maker, and natural leader. Bob Phillips, author of *The Delicate Art of Dancing with Porcupines,* labels them a driver, and the DISC test, dominant. Their primary shortcomings are a lack of empathy and their bulldozer mentality. They are so focused on the task at hand they can sometimes run over people to get it done. They are primarily motivated by POWER. Fun to them is anything *they* decide on. The best way to motivate a Choleric is to give him or her choices. This POWERFUL personality loves to be the hero.

Brock wrote an obituary for himself as a part of a junior high English assignment:

> Brock William Farrel was a model father. He died while saving his daughter from a car. His family was crossing the street in a crosswalk when a man in a white Porsche came speeding into the intersection. The driver did not see the pedestrians and almost hit Brock's little girl. Before the car hit her, Brock pushed her out of the way and took a direct hit from the car. He died five hours later in the hospital. "Life is 10 percent what happens to us and 90 percent how we react"—Vince Lombardi. (Then he added a PS:) "I think Brock acted the right way!"

I was amazed at how one short paragraph could provide so many clues into Brock's personality: He was a model father. Of course, model fathers make all the right decisions. He died a hero's death, providing for the safety of a loved one with quick-thinking action! He was hit by a white Porsche— a typical Choleric would say, "Well there are only a few real power and prestige cars. If you're going to go out, go out in style!" He quoted Vince Lombardi, one of the winningest football coaches in history. Then to make sure no one would get it wrong, he told us, "Brock made the right decision!"

The Popular

The other extrovert is the people-oriented Sanguine. Brawner labels these people Otters because they love to have fun. Phillips calls them expressive; the DISC, inspirational.

They are creative, spontaneous, and have super people skills! Their primary weaknesses are a lack of perseverance (if it isn't fun, why stay at it?); and they love a party, so they can seem shallow and flippant to some of the other personalities. They are primarily motivated by PEOPLE and PRAISE. All they want is a little ATTENTION—ok, a lot of attention, and they will do anything to get it. If you want to motivate a Sanguine, hook a task to a person or make it a party and they are there for you! It is important with this Popular personality to find positive, not negative, ways for them to get the attention they crave.

Zach has this personality style. When he was cast as the lead role in the school Christmas play, everyone thought the director had lost her mind. Zach, when he was in kindergarten, ran from the science fair to throw up just because he was supposed to hold up his insect collection and say one sentence about it! But Debe was so perceptive, she saw how he naturally was the part in his everyday life. He was flamboyant, liked to be the center of attention, was funny—he had just always felt that he might let someone down if he were to play a lead role, and to Zachery, nothing could be worse than to let down someone you loved. For years, our main aim was to convince him that if he was just who God made him, he'd never let us down. So when he was cast as the pharaoh, and got to act funny, make people laugh, and pleased his drama teacher and mom and dad—he was in heaven! All Debe had to do was tell him, "Zach, you are the best person for this part. I don't have anyone else who can come close to doing this part the way it needs to be done." The more Zach played the part, the more positive praise he received. By the end of the production, he was asked to do a promo piece at morning worship service. He even added in a line and, in character as the pharaoh, gave directions to his father who was standing in the pulpit! The congregation loved it, and the laughter just boosted his little ego all the more!

I have this personality trait, so I can easily understand why Zach makes some of the decisions he makes. I can also understand what will wound his spirit and set him back from achieving his potential. The people-pleaser aspect of this personality can cause severe paralysis. My main goal as Zach's mother is to help him tune into how he can please God—otherwise he will be tossed back and forth by public opinion or he will be frozen, afraid to risk because he might not please someone. However, when these personalities are in tune with the power that comes from pleasing God, they can become mighty tools of the kingdom because by nature they have great people skills and are master persuaders.

The Peaceful

The Phlegmatic, or Brawner's Retriever, is an introverted, no frills, peace-at-all-costs, likeable guy or gal. Phillips labels these as amiable; the DISC says they are steady. Everybody loves the Peaceful personality. Everyone gets along with them because they make it their goal in life not to rock the boat. Everyone likes them—unless you want something done or you need a decision out of them or you are in a hurry. Then they can drive you crazy! Caleb tests out almost even between Peaceful and the next personality style of Perfect.

It is impossible to rush Caleb in the morning. His favorite place to be is right next to Mom or Dad. And I mean right next to. He is like glue. He is a hug waiting to happen. He lives to make other people happy, and he is happiest when he feels emotionally close and connected with those he loves.

I got a clue when he was about three and we were driving around town. I was preoccupied by some discouraging news I had received. Caleb was sitting next to me in his car seat. He's a perceptive little guy. He said, "Mommy, what's wrong?"

Knowing the content of my problem was well over his head, I just said, "I have something on my mind, and I want to talk to Daddy about it."

"Where's Daddy?"

"Honey, he's in a meeting."

"Daddy is always in a meeting."

"Yes, that's a lot of what pastors do. They meet with people, talk with them about their problems, and help them find God's plans."

"When will Daddy not be in meetings?"

"I don't know, honey—"

"I do," he interrupted. "When all the people in the world are dead. Then there won't be any more meetings!"

His candor caught me off guard, and I couldn't help but laugh out loud. To which Caleb replied, "See, I knew I could make you happy."

I am also married to a man whose secondary personality is Peaceful. All that a Peaceful personality needs in life is to be appreciated. I know I could not do what I do as a leader, traveling speaker, and writer if Bill weren't in my life. He really is the wind beneath my wings. Even while writing this book I told him, "Honey, I need you. You are my inspiration," and I meant it. People just function better with a little TLC and the Peaceful personalities can give emotional support well.

The theme song of the Peaceful though would be Aretha Franklin's R-E-S-P-E-C-T! All they want is a little respect. When you show appreciation and respect to these people, they will do almost anything for you. It might take them a while, but they will get it done.

The Perfect

The Melancholy personality is introverted and task ori-
ented. Most great artists and musicians are this personality.
They are creative and they want things done right. They
have the patience to do things with excellence. Their perfec-
tionism can drive other people, primarily the Sanguine,
crazy. The Sanguine's response to a Melancholy will always
be, "Lighten up!" But they can't lighten up. The world is
black and white and is in desperate need of fixing to these
folks. They can become negative and depressed because
they see the glass half-empty and all the little undone things
in the world.

The Brawner model calls this person a Beaver because
they are hardworking and get the job done. The DISC test
calls them cautious, and Bob Phillips labels them as analyt-
ical. They are always thinking, processing. When Brock was
younger, I thought he might be like his father and have this
trait because he was so good at academics. But as he has
gotten older, I see the Lion's "the end justifies the means" in
him more often. Melancholys can never bring themselves to
cut corners.

My husband, Bill, is my editor. Because I am Sanguine
and Choleric, I can create ideas by the boatload, and I think
all of them are brilliant, of course, just because I came up
with them. I want to set sail with a host of ideas. Bill is my
rudder in life, helping me to sort through the ideas, choose
the best ones, and make them rise to the level of excellence.
Without him, my impatient personality (which comes from
both of my temperaments) would make many mistakes—
possibly a few tragic ones.

Parenting a Melancholy can be a mixed bag. They will
always be the ones with a clean room, but they might be
obsessive about it. One friend of mine with a Melancholy

son finally got a lock to put on the outside of his door because he could tell if someone had walked into his room! My sister has a little Melancholy in her—all her clothes had to hang on hangers the same color as the garments! (I was lucky if I remembered to hang mine up.) Sharing a room with her was great for me and horrible for her. Deney was constantly cleaning up behind me because she couldn't stand my haphazard ways. After all, who has time to organize a closet when there is a date to go on or a party to attend? Deney organized her books from tallest to smallest. She had bins and boxes for everything.

To motivate a Melancholy, you have to give them answers because they will ask, "Why do we have to do it? Why do we have to do it this way?" They like answers and structure. And don't deviate off the plan!

When you parent a Perfect, make very few promises or you will lose credibility. But create a plan, some rituals they can rely on, and you will be able to bring out the best in them.

Understanding the Factor of Birth Order

Dr. Kevin Leman in *The New Birth Order Book* gives us a short sample quiz to help the reader get a quick grasp of birth order:

Which of the following sets of personality traits fits you best?

> A. Perfectionist, reliable, conscientious, list-maker, well-organized, hard-driving, natural leader, critical, serious, scholarly, logical, doesn't like surprises, loves computers.
> B. Mediator, compromising, diplomatic, avoids conflict, independent, loyal to peers, many friends, a maverick, secretive, unspoiled.

C. Manipulative, charming, blames others, atten-
tion-seeker, tenacious, people person, natural
saleperson, precocious, engaging, affectionate,
loves surprises.

D. Little adult by age seven, very thorough, deliberate, high achiever, self-motivated, fearful, cautious, voracious reader, black-and-white thinker,
uses, "very," "extremely," "exactly" a lot, can't
bear to fail, has very high expectations for self,
more comfortable with people who are older or
younger.

If you noted that the test seemed rather easy
because A, B, C listed traits of the oldest right on down
to the youngest in the family, you are right. If you
picked list A, it's a very good bet you are firstborn in
your family. If you chose list B, chances are you are a
middle child....If list C seemed to relate best to who
you are, it's likely you are the baby in the family....But
what about list D? It describes the only child.[5]

Reading Dr. Leman's complete work is a good idea
because the basic traits of birth order can be impacted by
spacing between children, the sex of each child, physical,
mental, and emotional differences, sibling deaths, adoptions,
the birth order of each parent, and the blending of families.

Dr. Leman has done extensive research in this area. "For
example, statistics show that firstborns often fill positions of
high authority or achievement. *Who's Who in America* or
American Men and Women in Science both contain a high per-
centage of firstborns. You will also find them more than well
represented among Rhodes scholars and university presidents. As for presidents and pastors, you guessed it, a great
number of them are firstborns. The way I define firstborn,

twenty-three of forty of U.S. Presidents (56 percent) have been firstborn or functional firstborns."[6] (Note: An example of a functional firstborn is our newest president, George W. Bush, who is the oldest because the first son in the Bush family died very early in childhood.)

The first 23 of 25 astronauts sent into space by the U.S. were firstborns! (And then "at the other end of the birth order scale, you will find a lot of later borns who are comedians"![7])

The secondborn sees the older sibling as stronger, smarter, and bigger and will usually shoot off in a completely different direction from that of his or her sibling. The key is to provide direction so the secondborn doesn't look at his or her "perfect, high-achieving" sibling and decide the only identity is to be the "black sheep" of the family. Parents who make a conscientious effort to help each child see his or her uniqueness and value will be able to find a positive outlet for the second sibling.

In our family, when Zach entered junior high, he took up skateboarding. His older brother was totally inept at the sport, which made the sport even more attractive to Zach. He wrote all his English papers about skateboarding, his science fair was about skateboarding, he wore skater clothing, and he even launched his own line of "Zeek" wear. (The clothing motto was, "Don't be a geek, wear Zeek!") He even designed his own business cards for the company. We made sure he kept up his other interests, football, friendships, and guitar lessons, but he definitely identified with the skater crowd. We were careful to not allow him to "hang" with skaters. If he was going to skate, he was going to do it legally, safely, and competitively. Even though a few of our friends were concerned that all Zach wanted to talk about was skating, we knew at this point in time he needed something he felt he was really great at. And he was a really good skater. For Zach, having something he was great at and Brock wasn't was vital, especially as they were so close in age and he would really feel the shadow of Brock as he entered high school.

We even weighed all kinds of high school options for Zach and talked with him about whether the he felt he could make his own mark if he attended the same school as his brother. In the end, because Zach felt he had his own set of strengths that were different from his brother's, he chose to attend the same high school because they really are good friends.

Lastborns have an insatiable desire for attention (maybe because they have to fight for it under the shadow of so many siblings, or maybe because they are used to it being the "baby" of the family). This desire for attention makes the lastborn just bold enough to try almost anything. Dr. Leman, also a lastborn says, "We just go ahead and *do it* and worry about the repercussions later."[8]

A thumbnail sketch of considerations parents can make based on birth order is:

- *Firstborns need a break!* Because they are already hard on themselves, you don't need to be so hard on them. Because of their driver personality, you might want to go overboard in teaching them people skills like tact, empathy, and compassion to balance out the achiever in them. If they are also only children, expose them to relationships so they can learn important people skills like sharing, caring, peer-level interaction, and negotiation. Both firstborn and only children feel an intrinsic need to be perfect, so let them see your flaws and how you handle failure.

- *Middle children need understanding.* Give your middle children space to explore their feelings, their options, and their identity. If you have several middle children, don't let them get lost in the shuffle. Help them identify and build into their own unique gifts. Don't let every thing in their life be "hand-me-down." They have natural people skills, so let them use them. They may want more social time away from the family, and that's all right. It's one place they can feel like the "top dog."

♦ *Lastborns need structure.* Give your lastborn discipline and try to keep the same family rules. Even if you try to parent the same, you will naturally be a little easier on the lastborn just because you are more relaxed in your role as a parent. Don't make things too easy for the lastborn. Help them excel academically because everyone in the family is smarter than them just because of age. They have the confidence to tackle big challenges, so let them. Don't squelch their dreams.

Understanding How They Learn

I would highly recommend buying and marking up Cynthia Tobias' *The Way They Learn.* Cynthia, an educator, describes how children perceive the world and process information. She places children in four major categories:

(1) *Concrete Sequential:* those who are conventional, accurate, hardworking, factual, organized, and consistent learners; (2) *Abstract Sequential:* those who analyze well because they are structured, objective, logical, and systematic; (3) *Abstract Random:* those who are sensitive, compassionate, and imaginative and also prefer to be spontaneous and flexible; and (4) *Concrete Random:* those who are intuitive, curious, creative, instructive, adventurous—but realistic.[9]

Three Weddings, Three Personalities!

Carol Rischer and I were slated as the presenting team for a women's retreat that was in a remote community along the California coast, so we decided to drive the seven hours together. When we hit the topic of raising kids, she entertained me for hours as she described the differences in her three beautiful daughters' weddings. Here's a condensed picture of just how personality and birth order can combine for some very unique weddings!

"Melanie is our Choleric-Melancholy mix. She is Type A, responsible, and firstborn. She planned her wedding to neatly follow six weeks after her graduation from university. The production was elegant, formal, sophisticated, and dramatic—as is our Melanie. Her gown was elaborate, well beaded with ornate long sleeves and an appropriately dramatic long train. Her music featured a classical symphonic string quartet plus a trumpeter playing a trumpet voluntary as her processional. Melanie's pastor daddy officiated and included a tearful presentation from him of a pearl necklace to remind her of her value. The bride and the groom sang beautifully to each other in the tradition of her parents (that would be my husband and me back in 1969). The wedding dinner/dance/reception was poolside at a formal hotel setting where the surrounding hillside mountains were part of the planned backdrop for our out-of-town guests. Graciousness reigned. God balanced Melanie's responsible personality with a patient and nurturing psychologist husband who continues to listen, level, and lead in their Christian marriage.

"Cheryl, our Sanguine, fun-loving middle child planned a wedding celebration that was entitled 'The Wedding of a Gentleman and a Princess' and was scripted on the PowerPoint screens above the sanctuary. Cheryl's curiosity and flair for adventure led her to her man on the Christian Singles "Internet." Two adventuresome, godly Christian virgins somehow found each other! Cheryl's bridesmaids did a little skip dance step down the aisle to the jazzy 'It Had to Be You' and Cheryl 'twirled' down the aisle in her beaded, off-the-shoulder Princess gown with her daddy's arm raised above her head. Her music was a jazz combo—trumpet/keyboard/drums/guitar/bass—performed by professionals who added zest and vitality to an already exciting story. Cheryl surprised her groom at the reception by sitting him on a chair on the dance floor and singing to him Shania Twain's 'Any Man of Mine.' Rob surprised Cheryl with a dance rendition of a *Men in Black* routine with his guy friends. God knew Cheryl's 'life's a party' outlook would best be balanced with a stable corporate defense attorney who loves the Lord and his sparkling bride!" (Note the major change from wedding number one to wedding number two. Those secondborns don't want to fall into their older sibling's perfect shadow. Cheryl created a memory completely different. The Sanguine in her made the day one few people would ever forget!)

"Deanna, who is a Phlegmatic, Type B, nothing-is-worth-stressing-about baby of the family, married only 11 days after she arrived home from her university graduation and choir tour. She knew all the details would be taken care of—why wouldn't we all want to help her?—and that her wedding would be perfect. The stage was dramatic, with a dozen hand-painted pillars surrounded by a sea of candles. Deanna floated down the aisle—smiling and genuinely relaxed—in her simple but gorgeous gown—with her groom waiting anxiously for his life mate and ministry mate. They sang, emotionally but professionally, "From this Moment." Since they are both performers, both confident, they were both ready to enjoy every minute of the day and the rest of their lives. Their music was classic jazz with professional sax, bass, and piano. The dinner dance was a celebration for all to enjoy—none of this uptight stuff for them. God let the PK (pastor's kid) become a PW (pastor's wife) who will survive because she doesn't sweat the small stuff. She lets others worry about what they want to. The crowds cheered and blew bubbles as their limo drove off with the couple standing and waving to their fans through the sunroof. Life is to be enjoyed!" (Note the lastborn style. She knew everyone would want to be a part of pulling her wedding together in a short amount of time. The babies of the family can be very responsible like Deanna, but they also might take risks like pulling together a wedding from the road. Deanna was on tour just prior to her wedding! Lastborns who have a winning family know they have a terrific team who will all pull together to make the event wonderful—they always have! Lastborns know the system and work the system, and because they are so easy to be around and are such natural people people, everyone usually really enjoys being a part of their lives even if they have to do a little bit of the work!)

Cynthia also explains three educational terms for the way children best learn a body of information:

1. *Auditory Learners:* those who remember information best if they hear it. These children do best if they have parents who will:

- Offer to drill them verbally
- Help them put information into rhythmic patterns, like a song or rap
- Let them read aloud
- Minimize visual distractions in the study area
- Say out loud what is vital they know

2. *Visual Learners:* those who remember best if they have seen the information, not just heard it. These children perform best if their parents:

- Give them bright colors and large spaces to draw or write
- Encourage them to doodle or take notes while listening
- Let them underline or highlight in a book or draw symbols or pictures they can associate with vital facts or figures
- Provide charts, pictures, and graphs that help log the information in their minds

3. *Kinesthetic Learners:* those who learn by experience or touch. These children learn more easily if they:

- Take frequent breaks while studying
- Can write and draw in large spaces
- Hear stories aloud that have lots of action
- Move while learning, act out material, or even pace while memorizing[10]

As the parent of a kinesthetic learner (Zach), I can tell you traditional classrooms for the most part are not set up well to enhance their learning. Sitting still and having textbooks and worksheets, but little hands-on learning means that you might have to go out of your way to provide alternatives and options to help your child learn. We built skate ramps to learn math. Zach and I would go on walks where we talked through projects, papers, and test data. We bought all kinds of games to learn spelling, reading, math, history, and social studies information. Pulling in art and music seemed to add to Zach's ability to learn.

These learners can be seen as uncooperative in a classroom, but with some creative parenting and some creative teachers, these children can excel.

Understanding How They Perceive Love

Often as children become adults, they express frustration over certain choices their parents might have made. In families of several children, one episode might be *interpreted* many ways. The *perception* of love is as relevant to a child as the foundation of love itself. Children feel loved in a variety of ways. Gary Chapman contends there are five love languages: *Words of Affirmation, Physical Touch, Quality Time, Acts of Service,* and *Gifts.*[11] Of course, every person loves all these expressions of love; however, one or two might mean more to each of your children.

Chapman suggests three main tools to discover your child's love language: questions, observation, and experimentation. "Questions may be your greatest ally...you might ask, 'If you really wanted to show your grandmother you loved her, how would you do it?'" A child's or teen's answer might be a reflection of what speaks love to him or her. Chapman continues, "Look for ways in which he expresses love or appreciation to others. Keep notes on what you observe....Observe also the complaints of the teenager. What a person complains about is a clue to his or her primary love language."[12] Finally, Chapman says that a third way to discover a teenager's primary love language is to experiment by focusing on one of the five love languages each week and observe the teen's response. All in all, you can't go wrong if you parent by using all the love languages with all your children—then you are bound to be speaking love to each child somehow, someway!

◆　◆　◆

CAUGHT YOU BEING GOOD

One goal of parenthood is to help children get an accurate view of themselves from God's perspective. Not an inflated view, which some of today's educational methods might produce. For example, it does a child no favors to never give D's or F's. If a child is failing in a course, the parent, child, and teacher need a plan to address the problem, and the answer can't be just to pretend the problem doesn't exist for fear of hurting his or her feelings by giving out a poor mark. When that child gets out into the real world, an employer isn't going to stroke the child's ego just to get a job completed.

Children deserve to see what areas are their strengths so they can focus on those for their future, and they need to know weaknesses so you can create a plan to fortify and shore up those areas. Here are two great ideas from Emilie Barnes:

◆　In her More Hours in My Day seminars, Emilie explains how she gives stickers that say, "Caught You Being Good" to her grandchildren.

◆　She also has reward coupons that a parent can give for a job well done, and you can write in what the coupon can be redeemed for.

Look for ways to praise your child for being good and for a job well done. As you consciously try to praise and reward, you will begin to notice patterns of what each child is consistently getting praised for.[13]

7

THE KEY TO THE
TREASURE CHEST

Unleashing Potential Through Prayer

I have several prayer notebooks where I keep track of my prayer requests. Recently, I taught a six-week session called Woman's Prayer Project. We each gathered photos of those we loved and created scrapbook pages for each person that included verses we were going to pray over them and the requests, hopes, and dreams we had for each of them. It was a fun project, and the ladies can use the scrapbooks in their daily devotions.

I would encourage you to create a prayer book with photos of your children and requests you are praying. Add verses to pray along with the requests.

Fern Nichols, founder of Moms in Touch, created a photo album complete with all the verses, requests, answers, and pictures of answers for each of her children. She presented them to her kids—and it was the first thing each child packed as they left for college. It became a wonderful natural tool for sharing their faith on campus.

Swap Kid Concerns

Sometimes, if you have a prayer request for your child that seems to be the same one over and over, for years and years, it gets easy to start believing the lie, "Why bother, nothing's ever going to change." If you are feeling that way, approach another mom who has also been praying for her child for a long period of time. It can be easier to believe that God will move when you aren't as emotionally drained as you are for your own child. It's even easier to pray when they are different concerns. Maybe you are praying for a prodigal daughter and your friend has a son who hasn't made a decision for Christ yet. If you see change or movement in your friend's child's life, it can renew your own faith. It is easy to think that if you aren't getting immediate results that something must be wrong with your prayers. Exchanging requests can sometimes bolster your own faith and give you renewed strength to go the distance with your own child.

Much of my faith in God and belief in the power of prayer has come from women who mother under crisis. In my role as a pastor's wife I have stood clutching their hands as they have said goodbye at a graveside. I have been a sounding board when they have had to make tough decisions on surgeries, schooling, and sending them down the aisle. I have sat in classrooms, courtrooms, counseling rooms, and waiting rooms. I have seen how *strong* God can be on behalf of a parent. One of my favorite verses is 2 Timothy 2:13, "If we are faithless, he will remain faithful, for he cannot disown himself."

Over and over I have witnessed the faithfulness of God. I think one of the best gifts a parent can ever give a child is to have a strong personal faith in God, so that when our children need us to believe God for something big in their lives, we have the faith to loan to them.

One of the examples of strong faith I have pinned up on the bulletin board of my soul is my friend Julie. Her daughter Sarah was born with her skull not fully developed. All babies have soft spots, but Sarah's was much worse. It refused to close. Doctors weren't sure Sarah would live. But she was a fighter, and she pulled through—but Julie had to make sure that Sarah never bumped her head and never cried. Now that is stress!

When Sarah was about three, she had to go in for major surgery. Their family was a part of our local church, and many of us gathered for a prayer and worship service on Sarah's behalf. A prayer chain was coordinated. One of the gifts Julie gave each of us was a prayer card for her daughter. Each card had a picture of Sarah on it and a Bible verse that Julie asked that we pray for Sarah each time we looked at it. I placed mine on the refrigerator where it has remained to this day. I still pray for Sarah even though she is a beautiful blonde walking miracle. She is now nearly a teen, and she had survived numerous surgeries and hospital stays.

A parent of less faith might have coddled or spoiled such a sick child, but Julie has done all she can to integrate Sarah and normalize her life. And that's been a challenge. Sarah can never be without one of her parents because her medical condition is so complicated and tenuous. She cannot be bumped or hit, so there is no roughhousing for her. She cannot participate in an activity where she could fall. But if you met her, you wouldn't know this. She is vivacious, sweet, personable, and sings like an angel.

Every parent of a special-needs child has a moment, a crisis of faith where they are at a crossroad. They can either become bitter and angry at God and question, "Why us?" or they can by faith reach out for the hem of Christ's garment and trust that in doing so, some of His power might be available on behalf of their family and their child. Julie has done that. Her faith is like a giant sequoia tree. It is silent, majestic, and strong. Just gazing at it, one would have the same response as standing at the base of those giant, beautiful trees, an awe and a wonder at the God who could create something so beautiful, yet so strong.

In *The Power of a Praying Parent,* Stormie Omartian writes,

> We don't have to pace the floor anxiously, biting our nails, cracking our knuckles, dreading the terrible twos or tortuous teens. We don't have to live in fear of what each new development may bring, what dangers might be lurking behind every corner. Nor do we have to be perfect parents. We can start right now—this very minute, in fact—making a positive difference in our child's future. It's never too early and it's never too late....The key is not trying to do it all by ourselves all at once, but rather turning to the expert parent of all time—our Father God—for help....There is great *power* in doing that, far beyond what most people imagine.[1]

I have found that what prayer accomplishes more than anything else is a change in me! That's why I have decided to pray before I *push,* pray before I *panic,* pray before I *pressure.* One of the mothers in my prayer circle reminds herself: *Pray it, don't say it!*

When you pray first, then, if and when God leads you to confront a situation, you act and react more like God, and He can parent through you. Prayer turns your heart into a vessel of His love and discernment. To remind me of my commitment to pray first, I often wear a bracelet that says: P.U.S.H. (Pray Until Something Happens!)

Personalizing Prayer

One of my favorite ways to pray is to pray Scripture, personalizing it for the child I am praying for. There are a couple of ways to do this. One is very simple. Just choose a portion of Scripture (the psalms work well) that hits some of the areas you are concerned for your son or daughter.

For example, last year, the night before Brock's football games, I would pray a section of Psalm 91 over Brock. I simply would pray as I scratched his back, or with just my hand on his shoulder, whatever seemed most natural at the moment. Here's a portion of a personalized version of Psalm 91:

> Brock, who dwells in the shelter of the Most High, will rest in the shadow of the Almighty. Brock will say of the Lord, "He is my refuge and my fortress, my God, in whom I trust." Surely God will save you from the fowler's snare and from the deadly pestilence. He will cover Brock with his feathers, and under his wings you will find refuge; his faithfulness will be Brock's shield and rampart....If Brock makes the Most High his dwelling—even the Lord, who is your refuge—then no harm will befall you, no disaster will come near your tent. For he will command his angels concerning you, Brock, to guard you in all your ways...."Because Brock loves me," says the Lord, "I will rescue him; I

will protect him, for he acknowledges my name. He will call upon me, and I will answer him; I will be with him in trouble, I will deliver him and honor him."

The other option is to create a composite of verses that fortifies an area of weakness. If you have a concordance, you can look up verses by finding key words that might be in the verse in that subject area. For example, all of my children have been afraid of the dark or have had nightmares. I have taught them how to take their stand in Christ and say, "In the name of Jesus and His shed blood on the cross, I command any evil spirits be silenced and sent away." Then I encourage them to pray the truth about God's power, victory, and ability to overcome (inserting their name in the blanks):

> You, dear_____, are from God and have overcome them, because the one who is in you is greater than the one who is in the world (1 John 4:4). For he has rescued _____ from the dominion of darkness and brought _____ into the kingdom of the Son he loves (Colossians 1:13). "I have told you these things, so that in me you may have peace. In this world you will have trouble. But take heart! I have overcome the world" (John 16:33). I write to _____, because you are strong, and the word of God lives in you, and you have overcome the evil one (1 John 2:14). With God we will gain the victory, and he will trample down our enemies (Psalm 108:13). But thanks be to God! He gives _____ the victory through our Lord Jesus Christ (1 Corinthians 15:57). Everyone born of God overcomes the world. This is the victory that has overcome the world, even our faith (1 John 5:4).

Experiencing the Power of Prayer

I love to pray using God's Word because you never know what day you might need it. I had begun to pray for Caleb before he was born, but my biggest answer to prayer for him was quite dramatic. It was life changing for the both of us.

I had been out running errands. As I walked into the house the phone was ringing. It was the phone call that no mother ever wants to receive. "Pam," said a voice I barely recognized as Bill's. He sounded scared and he struggled with the words he was weighing out. "The sheriff wants you to bring as many photos of Caleb as you can find. Honey, the boys are missing."

I hung up the phone and burst into tears. My Caleb was only five years old! How could he be missing? He had been at his best friend's house playing, and now he and his little friend were gone.

I looked around for photos of Caleb but I couldn't see any. My eyes blurred with tears of panic. *God, Caleb needs me right now. I need to find pictures. Please be with my Caleb, and help me be the kind of mom he needs. Give me your peace.*

A supernatural calm came over me, and as I looked up I could see that there were photos of Caleb all over the wall and albums of them on the shelf. I grabbed them and ran out the door.

As I headed across town, I panicked again. *Oh, God, what was he wearing? What did I put on him this morning? I* couldn't remember. *I must be a terrible mother! I can't even remember what I put on my little boy! God, I need your peace! I can't think. Please help me be the kind of mom Caleb needs. Help me remember. Give me peace so I can think. What did I put on him for kindergarten? Protect Caleb, give him peace.*

Then I remembered: striped shirt, black sweatpants, brown boots. Tears puddled in my eyes and overflowed down my cheeks. I blinked and frantically wiped my eyes because I couldn't see the road.

Lord, give me Your peace. Help me make it to Gail's.

I thought of my friend Gail, and I empathized with how frantic she must be feeling as well. What would I say to her? I knew she was a great mom, attentive and caring. *She's as freaked out as I am right now,* I thought. *God, what am I going to say to Gail? Give her peace. Help me be the kind of friend I need to be right now. Be with our two little boys. Give them Your peace.*

As I turned the corner, I saw Gail in the center of her yard. I parked the car and ran to wrap my arms around her. "Gail, I love you. We will get through this together. We'll pray, and God will find those boys." We begged God to watch over our children and to give us peace so we could think. Patrol cars were speeding to the scene, my husband appeared from behind the house. "Not there, either." Then he saw me. He wrapped his arms around me and he prayed, "God, help us find our precious Caleb."

The sheriff interrupted. "We are sending out all available squad cars and they have dispatched two helicopters. Are those the pictures of your children?" He asked a few more questions, then said, "We would like one parent of each child to stay with me at the command post." Bill suggested that the mothers stay, and he volunteered to lead the charge into the countryside of overgrown brush.

My older two boys went together through the neighborhood and caught kids coming off school buses to tell them, and soon more worried parents appeared from their homes to help in the search. When Brock and Zach returned, I sent one of my best friends home with them in case Caleb was going to try to make it home, five miles away. As they pulled from the curb, I could see their worried faces peering back at me. They were trying to be brave, but I knew they were anxious. As I watched the van pull around the corner and out of my sight, I was distressed because now I couldn't see anyone in my family. Even though I knew intellectually that my older boys would be safe with my friend, panic and fear began to rise again. *Lord, please give Brock and Zach peace. I can't see them or Bill, and they can't see me. And Caleb can't see any of us! We all need Your peace!*

The sheriff in command said, "Mrs. Farrel, what time is it?" I told him. It had already been two hours. Two helicopters appeared overhead. They announced like a booming voice from heaven, "Two missing youths, age five. Caleb Farrel..." Then they announced a description of each. I looked at Gail. Tears were streaming down both our faces. This was real. This was a nightmare.

God, be with Caleb. I know Your Word. You say You hem him in before and behind. You say all things are held in the palm of Your hand. You say that all the angels are at Your command. Send Your angels. Put a hedge of protection around those boys. Be with my Caleb. He knows You. Your Spirit resides inside him. Give him Your peace. Wrap Your love around him. And be with Bill too. Give him Your peace.

I pictured Bill, walking through that tall bushland around our city. Helicopters hovered overhead. It felt like a snapshot from Vietnam clips I had grown up seeing. Men died there. I came face-to-face with my worst fears and again prayed for Caleb. *Let Your presence be a shelter to him. Lord, You say You shelter us under Your wings, shelter Caleb. You say You are a fortress and a deliverer. Deliver Caleb.* I shook my head and prayed, *God, give me Your peace. Help me be the kind of mom I need to be. It won't help anyone if I break down. Give me Your peace, Your strength, Your hope. Give me YOU!*

A supernatural calm reassured my heart. I began to pray specifically for Caleb, imagining how he must feel.

"Mrs. Farrel, what time is it?" I told the officer. Now it had been over three hours. I began to cry as I sensed the precious time ebbing away.

I prayed, *God, You know all things. I take my stand in You and Your shed blood on the cross. I command all evil be sent away through Your power.* The peace returned and I continued to pray for Caleb and direct the stream of new volunteers that kept arriving.

"Mrs. Farrel, what time is it?"

I wanted to scream, "Get a watch!" But I didn't. I prayed, *Help me be the kind of citizen I need to be right now.* So I looked at my watch and again told the officer the time.

"It's been four hours. If we don't find the boys in the next few minutes, we will have to go down the street to the fire station and set up a permanent command post."

The words slapped me in the face. I knew what that meant, and it was not good news. I'd seen all the John Walsh films, I'd showed *Stranger Danger* and all those kinds of videos to my children. This was bad news. This was the loss of hope. This was the beginning of the end.

God, You say You are in control, and I believe that. I am going to choose right now, that no matter what happens, that I will hang on to You. I've seen families go through tragedy. The families that make it have chosen You. I know statistics say that the death of a child means the break up of over 90 percent of marriages that experience that trauma. I know that the only hope and help for my family is to believe You are who You say You are. Lord, Your Word says You are good and You are wholly good. It says You can turn dark into light and work all things together for good, so right now I am choosing to believe that. And even if they bring my precious Caleb to me dead across their arms, I will choose to believe the truth of who You are. It is the only hope. I can choose despair or I can choose You. I choose You. Give us Your presence—Caleb, Bill, Brock, Zach, and me. I am claiming and standing in Your peace.

A voice shook me from my daze of prayer. I saw a squad car pull up and two officers talking. The commander approached, "We have received a sighting of two youths. We are sending a squad car by to see if the two children are your sons. We don't yet have confirmation..."

I smiled and said, "But we have hope." The time... ticked...slowly...by...so Gail and I prayed some more together and God held us together with His peace. About 20 minutes later, a squad car pulled up. Two doors popped open and out tumbled two tousled, dirty, ragtag boys—*our boys!* I ran to my son, wrapped my arms around him, and said, "I love you, Caleb!"

I heard a quiet but relieved, "I love you, Mommy." Bill had run back at the news. He gave Caleb a hug and exchanged "I love you's" and then we said, "Where have you been?"

The story goes something like this: Caleb and his friend were eating fresh-baked cookies on Gail's front patio. Gail went in to get the last batch of cookies out of the oven. Her oven and where the boys sat were just a few feet from each other. When she returned, the boys were gone. She had looked everywhere. Finally, Bill had called her from school. The kindergartners got out earlier than the rest of the school, so often they would go to each other's homes to play and then return back to school when their siblings got out for the day. That had been the plan. When Bill called Gail, she said, "I can't find the boys. I've looked everywhere. I've just called the police." Bill went immediately to Gail's and the police had already arrived. That's when he called me.

It seems that Caleb's friend had said to Caleb, "You want to go on a great adventure?" It was a simple game they played at school. They would simply march around the property pretending to be on some great Indiana Jones–type adventure. Caleb said, "Sure," and off they went. Around the corner, down a few blocks, and past Carol's, the block captain's home. Carol normally would have been stepping outside to go pick up her children from school, but she was pregnant and not feeling well when the boys traveled past her door. They came across some playground equipment at an apartment complex on their journey and played there for a while. The boys then looked up and Caleb's friend saw a mobile home park across the street and said, "My baby-sitter lives there! Let's go see her." (His sitter lives in a mobile home park in another city!) But the boys headed on over. They waited at the light at the busiest four-lane road in our community, and when it turned green they sped across the street and played in some people's yards, and then went underground into a huge storm tunnel. That's where they were for all those hours.

We're not sure whether they got tired, hungry, afraid, had to go to the bathroom, or all of the above, but eventually they popped their heads out from the storm drain. The manager of the mobile home park, a kindly grandmother, had rallied the retirees of the park and everyone was out looking for our two boys. When she saw them, she said, "Now boys, I think your parents are very worried about you. Why don't we get into my golf cart and go call the police so you can get back to them?"

My son piped up, "Oh ma'am, we can't get in your golf cart. You're a stranger." (He can totally run away from home for over four hours when he's never even been allowed to go out of the front yard before, but he had been trained to say no to strangers!) Just then, a parent from our school drove in the park and saw what was happening. He got out of the car, with his daughter whom they knew, and said, "Hi, guys. You know me, you know my daughter. Why don't we ALL get in the golf cart and go call the police!"

That was the longest day of my life—but God gave me peace. I am a different mother because of that day. And Caleb is a different young man. A few days after his ninth birthday, Caleb said to me, "Mom, last weekend, did you share with the women at the retreat the story of when I got lost?"

"Yes, honey. It helps their faith in God grow."

"Like it did mine. It's like God saved me for something important, and I just need to stay close to Him and He'll show me, right?"

"Right." *So right.*

God has a plan for Caleb, and for your child, and for you. I have experienced how He works all together for my good. I know God can get me through anything involving my children. I have a sure confidence, a proven faith. I also treasure each and every moment. I treasure the mundane task of folding a million sets of white athletic socks. I love to run my fingers through Caleb's curly hair. I get less frustrated over the small stuff, like plates left on the coffee table, burps, or the mountains of sneakers, cleats, and sports bottles that reappear across the living room each day. I treasure the privilege of just seeing each child, of serving each child, of praying for each child, and of being inconvenienced and annoyed by each child. The treasure is so much sweeter after having come close to losing it.

◆   ◆   ◆

A PRAYER FOR MY CHILDREN

Lord, I pray that my children will love You with all their heart, soul, mind, and strength and that Your Word will be on their hearts. Help me teach them diligently as we sit in our house, and when we walk and when we lie down and when we rise up. Help me find ways to bind them as signs on their hands and on their foreheads. Give me creative ways to place them on our doorposts and on our gates (Deuteronomy 6:7-9). Help them be strong and very courageous, being careful to do all according to Your law. Do not let them turn from the left or the right, so they might have success wherever they go. Help them be strong and courageous. Help them not to tremble or be dismayed, for You are with them wherever they go (Joshua 1:7-9). Let our home be like the people Joshua led, who said, "We will serve the LORD our God and obey him" (Joshua 24:24). Let Your gracious hand be on them (Nehemiah 2:8) and let them be prepared for such a time as this (Esther 4:14). Let them say, if the need arises that they should have to risk for You, "If I perish, I perish" (Esther 4:16). Let them choose to be blessed because they delight in Your law and meditate on it day and night. Make them like a tree firmly planted and which yields fruit in its season and in whatever they do, may they prosper (Psalm 1:3). Let them know that no good thing do You withhold from those who walk uprightly (Psalm 84:11 NASB). Help them continually set You before their eyes (Psalm 16:8).

Show them the path of life and that in Your presence is fullness of joy and pleasures forever (Psalm 16:11). Lord, be their rock of refuge and a strong fortress (Psalm 31:2). Let them trust in You and do good, dwell in the land and cultivate faithfulness, let them delight themselves in You and You will give them the desires of their hearts. Help them commit their way to You (Psalm 37:3-5). Let them trust in You with all their hearts and lean not on their own understanding. In all their ways help them acknowledge You and look to You as You make their paths straight (Proverbs 3:5-6).

But if they say, "I will not remember Him," let them feel like Jeremiah and say, "His Word is in my heart like a fire... I am weary of holding it in... I cannot" (Jeremiah 20:9). Let them shrink not from declaring the whole counsel of God (Act 20:27 KJV).

I know this will be true if they will present themselves to You as a living and holy sacrifice and not be conformed to this world, but be transformed by the renewing of their minds (Romans 12:2). Let them be wise in what is good and innocent in what is evil (Romans 16:19). Let them be patient and kind, not jealous or arrogant or unloving. Help them rejoice in the truth (1 Corinthians 13:4-6). Let them be filled with Your Spirit so they experience the fruit of love, joy, peace, patience, kindness, goodness, faithfulness, gentleness, and self-control (Galatians 5:22). I pray that the eyes of their hearts will be enlightened so that they will know what the hope of Your calling is, what the riches of glory Your inheritance in the saints are, and the surpassing greatness of Your power toward us who believe (Ephesians 1:18,19). Let them remember that they can do all things through You who strengthens them (Philippians 4:13), and let me say that I have no greater joy than this, than to hear of my children walking in the truth (3 John 4).

8

THE TREASURE IS BURIED

Triumphant Treasure
Amidst Life's Trials

Pass the buck, submit your resignation, withdraw your candidacy, revoke your permit, pull out of the race—isn't there *something* a parent can do to quit? What parent hasn't felt this at least once?

- ◆ When the call comes in the middle of the night...
- ◆ When the doctor says, "I'm afraid..."
- ◆ When a police officer shows up at your door...
- ◆ When your child says...
    ... I'm pregnant
    ... I'm gay
    ... I'm living with my boyfriend
    ... I don't believe in God
- ◆ When you've tried everything to get your child well and you're told, "This is as good as it gets."

156 THE TREASURE INSIDE YOUR CHILD

Parenting can feel so overwhelming and heartbreaking that at times you feel like you want out!

Sorry, not an option.

So if opting out doesn't work, what is a parent to do? What if the treasure in your child seems buried under an avalanche of special needs? Or what if your child has purposely buried the treasure within by becoming a prodigal and running from God?

A Genuine Original

In the movie *Indiana Jones and the Temple of Doom*, the main character endures all kinds of frightening episodes on his way to finding the treasure: an earthquake, snakes, spiders, robbers, and obstacles of every shape and size. Finally, he must step off a cliff and trust that a bridge will magically appear to carry him to safety on the other side. He has to take a step of faith.

Is that how you feel? Do you feel as though you have been running a marathon obstacle course and now God is asking you to step off a cliff into the unknown?

If you are the parent of a special needs child, you might feel like this every day.

How can a parent of a special needs child find the tools and the strength to uncover that special, unique, one-of-a-kind treasure that only your son or daughter can bring into the world?

Louise Tucker Jones, mother of a Down syndrome son, and coauthor Cheri Fuller give a few words of wisdom in *Extraordinary Kids: Nurturing and Championing Your Child with Special Needs*. Advice from parents who've been there includes:

◆ Be kind to yourself. Give yourself time to adjust. Let the other spouse have the freedom to not be where you are emotionally. Pamper yourself when stress hits.

◆ Pray for yourself and for wisdom to lead your child in the right path and not block God's plan for your child.

◆ Don't feel like you have to explain everything to everyone.

◆ Don't look too far forward or too far backward. Concentrate on today.

◆ Be honest with your feelings.

◆ You have lost an expectation, but you have gained a child.

◆ Lay any negative diagnosis at His (Jesus') feet, and listen for His direction.

◆ Don't let fear of a disability, an illness, or the future rule your life. God is sovereign![1]

This year, I had the great fortune to meet a truly amazing mother named Cricket. (With a name like Cricket, she was destined to make a mark in this world!) Her son, Matthew, was born severely disabled, but Cricket decided that every day, she would look for God's special blessing. It might be a small thing: a smile, a new movement, something that would say to her heart, "Matthew matters." She tenaciously journaled her feelings, his medical diagnosis, medications, advice, and resources. And in all those pages and pages of text, one story rises above the rest, the day Matthew did what no one else in the world could do.

A young man, Justin, has been attending our church for several months as he recently has been reunited with his father and new stepmother. He has always been EXTREMELY standoffish with everyone. Many of the students in the youth group have made efforts to get him involved and be his friend, but he pretty much has nothing to do with anyone. He often is seen by himself, not interested at all. The youth pastor and the adult team workers have all tried and been unsuccessful in getting him to do much of anything other than show up.

Justin, in appearance is somewhat intimidating and scary. He tends to dress all in black. His hair is shoulder length and usually greasy looking. He always has dog chains all over his body, around his neck, and hanging off his clothes, attached in a variety of places. This makes him a challenge to approach.

Well, Matthew was linked up with Michael, one of the teen buddies I arranged to accompany my son as he mainstreamed into the youth group. The two of them were sitting in the back row together, Michael in a chair and Matthew in his wheelchair next to him. Justin was standing several feet away, off by himself. Matthew suddenly wanted something out of his backpack hanging on the back of his chair. I assisted in unzipping the bag and then walked away, allowing a more natural procession to happen. Matthew desired Michael to get his snack. Michael looked at me for direction, and I signaled for him to tell Matthew no. Michael signed "no" to Matthew.

Matthew then wheeled himself over to Justin and grabbed his hand and wheeled them back to the back row. Then Matthew manipulated Justin's hand into the back of his backpack. Justin was then shown by Matthew to search for something! The search came to an end upon the discovery of a snack. Then, a spoon needed to be located. I helped with that. The rest was unbelievable. Matthew had Justin assist him in eating his entire snack. So Matthew is sitting between two young men, holding on to Michael's hand with his left hand and letting Justin feed him on the right.

A couple of times Michael would explain to Justin that Matthew could really feed himself. Justin held the container and Matthew would get the snack himself. It was the first time any of us have seen Justin interact with *anyone* or say anything to *anyone*. I encouraged him and thanked him repeatedly and attempted to make him feel very special.

In the middle of the encounter, I walked over to the youth pastor and said, "Don't look now, but a miracle is happening. It's the unlikely that will reach the unlikely."

A few weeks later, I asked Justin if he would consider being a buddy to Matthew while he played Challenge Little League. We offered to pick Justin up and drive him home and we would pay him. The two became baseball buddies—on and off the field.

Matthew reached a soul no pastor, parent, or peer could reach. Often special needs children change the world by changing us.

Working Through Grief

When a diagnosis comes that your child might have special needs, there is a loss of a dream. You will experience grief as you would any loss. Some stages of grief you might experience are:

◆ *Denial.* I can't believe this is happening to me.

- *Anxiety.* How can I possibly handle this?
- *Fear.* What will happen to my child and my family?
- *Guilt.* What did I do to cause this?
- *Depression.* My hopes and dreams seem lost forever.
- *Anger.* This isn't fair.
- *Acceptance.* I don't like what has happened. I don't understand why it happened. I don't know how I'm going to handle this. But God knows, and I can trust Him.[2]

Martha Little, mother of a child with special needs, offers the following steps to acceptance:

- *Acknowledge* that God's hand was on your child or children in the way they were formed before birth, according to His plan.
- *Admit* any areas you resent in the way God made them.
- *Accept* God's design for them. Thank Him for their personalities and the way they are.
- *Affirm* God's purpose in creating them for His glory.
- *Ally* yourself with God in His plans for them.[3]

Look for the Treasure

Prayerfully ask God to show you different forms of treasure:

The Treasure of Camaraderie. Find other parents who have children with the same or similar needs. There are support groups, online chat rooms, and parents in the same hospital or school that can empathize with you. Look for those who are positive—not chipper—and who tenaciously hold out hope and perseverance.

The Treasure of Knowledge. The more you know, the easier decision making will be. Invest in resources. A great start is the book *Extraordinary Kids* by Cheri Fuller and Louise Tucker Jones.

The Treasure of an Advocate. Connect with organizations or groups that specialize in helping children like your child.

The Treasure of Care. Plant yourself in a supportive church. Don't just look at one that might meet your child's need, look for one to meet your own. The stronger you are, the stronger you will be for your child.

The Treasure of Hope. Decide, before God, that somehow, someway you will look for the special blessing He will send your way each day.

Persevering with the Prodigal

Dealing with a prodigal can be heartbreaking. Jan, mom to Jordan, a promiscuous suicidal teen, explains, "It felt like I was watching her die slowly and nothing I could say or do seemed to matter. She even told me, 'Mom, you can't save me, so stop trying.'"

Of course Jan didn't stop trying. She never gave up on her daughter or the promise that "He who began a good work in Jordan will be faithful to complete it" (Philippians 1:6, paraphrased). How can you hang in with a prodigal and provide the unique parenting needed to help them stay in pursuit of the treasure God has placed inside?

Get Yourself Together

Jasmine, whose daughter was pregnant outside of marriage, said, "My daughter relied heavily on me during her crisis because she knew I was in constant contact with God, and she trusted my advice and guidance." Jasmine recommends that you "take every opportunity to grow in the Lord yourself. Feed yourself every day with God's Word through reading and studying the Bible, reading Christian books and magazines, and listening to Christian radio and music."

Renee, whose daughter suffered from chronic depression and then chose to seek affection in a sexual relationship when 15, discovered her daughter was pregnant. Renee gathered the two families to pray.

Though Renee felt like retreating, instead she obeyed God's call on her own life. "Don't retreat—serve! Be prepared to help others. Keeping our focus on serving Christ is essential." Lana, mother of two wayward young adults, one who is now on the mission field and one who is on his way back in a recovery center, agrees: "The natural situation isolates because of shame or embarrassment, but the biblical mandate is fellowship. It's natural to want to reject or run away, but God asks us to *embrace* the pain. Naturally I want to become angry or frustrated because of the lack of control, but biblically, God asks me to be a channel of love and forgiveness."

Helping others helps parents in pain. Toward the third trimester of her daughter's pregnancy, Renee began to find out about other families in the church who were experiencing a similar heartache. "I would drop a card of encouragement with my phone number for the mother. I began volunteering at the local crisis pregnancy care clinic. I became the liaison for our church where we 'adopted' an unwed teen mom-to-be and encouraged her and her mother through the pregnancy." Renee's daughter Pam had a short turnaround, during which time she married the baby's father, a strong Christian young man, and they moved into an apartment at her parents'. The couple stabilized, and Pam discovered she was pregnant again. Unfortunately, after the second baby was born, Pam abandoned her husband and children. Renee's son-in-law has stayed, and he is a good caring father who is finishing his education.

Renee's determination to stay strong in her own walk with God helped her gain a broader perspective of all the circumstances that have taken place. For years, Renee prayed that God would bring her husband to know Christ, and it was the trauma of having a daughter in crisis that brought a crisis to her own husband. He realized the only way he and the rest of his family would survive would be to lean on God's strength and power, not his own, so he began a personal relationship with Christ.

"My husband is transformed! My marriage is transformed for the better! What Satan meant for evil, God meant for good. All the prayers aren't answered for my daughter—yet—but I am confident that God continues to work His plan for our family and that plan will bring us a future and a hope."

Lana, a mom whose sons had a medical problem that encumbered their bonding as small children, has had a long journey parenting special needs children who also became prodigals for a period. She shares her secret for strength for the journey:

> The biggest thing is having a heavenly perspective, trying to see what God is seeing rather than my earthly perspective. God has shown this perspective primarily through the Word. When I took my eyes off Him, I used to dread getting up and every day seemed to be a battle. What began as survival, being in the Word just to survive each day, now has grown in heavenly perspective to a place where I am now willing to

endure the fellowship of Christ's sufferings in order to bring the greater glory of God. For example, if God will get the greater glory by me waiting one, two, three, or more years before solving the problem, I am now willing to wait.

Strength came from having a Scripture passage that I am meditating on, focusing on, that I pray and ask, "God give me your heavenly perspective." My world has grown to be more God-centered and less self-centered. It's been a long journey. When you are under ongoing pressure, God does a deeper work. Diamonds are made under pressure. I am liking the person I am becoming despite the stresses of the situation with my son.

Get a Team Together

Find a team for you. Most of the mothers surveyed recommended joining a Moms in Touch group. This national organization has groups in most cities representing almost every school. Groups of mothers gather to pray for each school. There are Moms in Touch groups for elementary years through college, and in some cities a "Moms Still in Touch" for prodigal children who might not even be in school anymore because of their choices.

Jasmine was in pain one Moms in Touch morning:

> The week before Thanksgiving, Leslie came to me and told me she was pregnant. Unbelievably I found myself not encouraging her in the way she had been raised, which is pro-life, but I encouraged her in her first initial response, which was to have an abortion out of fear of her dad's wrath. These talks on abortion and making an appointment took place between Monday and Friday of that week. Friday of that same week, I went to my Moms in Touch group. Asking for

prayer, I poured out my heart and shared how I was NOT guiding my daughter in the way that I should, and I cried.

One mom shared how she was a mother of an adopted son and what a blessing her child has been to both her and her husband. Another mom, with five children, poured out her heart on how precious her children have been and how precious is the gift of life. A third mom asked, "Jasmine, if her dad would support Leslie and help her through this crisis, would you be pushing for the abortion?" Absolutely not!

From that Friday morning God led us down the road of life—step by step, hour by hour, day by day, week by week, month by month. Every Friday at my Moms in Touch group we prayed specific prayers for Leslie. God answered within 24 hours by bringing our family to the next stepping-stone. We were experiencing incredible victories every week! By February it was truly becoming a celebration of life, not only for Leslie and me, but for everyone who was watching and praying for us.

Her father and I told Leslie we would support, love, and encourage her through her crisis pregnancy; however, if she chose to keep her baby, she would need to have her own apartment and raise her child on her own. She and her baby would not be able to live in our home. We recognized her time of rebellion was out of God's will and out of order.

Leslie chose to make a plan for an adoption. However, when the first family pulled out in April, she thought perhaps God was saying she should keep her child. She spent a week searching for resources to see if it would be feasible to raise her baby, continue her education, live in her own apartment, and work. And though she discovered she could with the vast amount of resources that are available to single mothers, Leslie came to me after that week and said, "Mom, one thing the government cannot provide for my baby is a dad."

Leslie turned to God again and realized that His plan for the baby and her was an adoption.

Through our Moms in Touch prayers God was able to bring Leslie's heart and head into one accord. Leslie knew this wasn't the right time in her life to have a baby, but that this baby was meant for another family.

The Lord brought a very special Christ-centered couple to Leslie, and she spent her last trimester building a relationship and creating an extended family with them. Kelly Anne was born on July 20, 1999 (my birthday). What an incredible day!

Renee, mom of four, one a prodigal, says, "Meeting each week with Moms in Touch moms gave me focus. It keeps my eyes on Jesus. What I gain is:

- *Direction.* This group encourages me to seek God always.
- *Support.* They pray for my daughter and for me.
- *Hope.* I am reminded God is faithful to answer the prayers of a righteous woman.
- *Strength.* Knowing I can call on others to join me at anytime is a real comfort. It is like a triple-braided cord. Their prayers give strength to my own."

Get a Team for Your Child

Jan said others were better at reaching the heart of Jordan than she was at times. "The greatest source of strength came from friends I had that loved Jordan without judging her. I needed to hear others say that they believed in her too. One of the things in her life that made a huge difference were the godly mentors who were in place at the time Jordan took her left turn. They were friends of hers and mine who cared about her and continued to keep in contact with her. At first this was hard for me because it felt like she trusted them more than me and she was confiding only in them, but as time went on, I realized that God had provided these friends to love her through a very difficult time." Later, Jordan shared that there are times in a prodigal's life when they aren't ready to come back because they want control of their lives and choices, but they are feeling God draw them back. Confiding in their parents would risk too much of the control, or they might feel they would hurt or disappoint their parents more. The friends served as a kind of testing ground or oasis on their journey home.

Jan continues, "There was a time when Jordan felt so hopeless that she actually had planned out her own suicide. It was to be on a Monday. The weekend prior to that Monday, our church youth group was going on a weekend retreat. To my surprise, Jordan wanted to go. I prayed continually the entire weekend that something that she heard would change her life. She called me the first evening to say she was bored. My heart sank, but I continued to pray. The next day Jordan felt God was leading her forward during the altar call to rededicate her life to Christ. She might not have had the courage but Rochelle, one of those godly mentors, had been there to walk down with her."

Moms of pregnant daughters are very grateful for other mothers, grandmothers, and family members who extend themselves to ask about the baby, throw baby showers, and extend a listening ear. Renee shares, "One night at church the elderly women at our church spontaneously gathered around my daughter to encourage her and pray for her. Our pastor at that time would request prayer for her and her new husband and the coming baby. He counseled them and announced the birth of our grandson."

Sandy, who had a drug-using runaway son, prayed, "God, run him down to get him the help he needs." That day the pastor of his church almost hit him with his car as the boy darted across traffic! The pastor recognized him and took him to breakfast, then called Sandy so she'd know her son was all right—and that God was watching out for him!

Get Resources Together

Lana advises, "Don't isolate! You need to find other people who have walked the path before you. Whatever the struggle is doesn't matter. You just need parents who have been there. Even some secular groups that have expertise can be helpful. Look for people in successful programs and look early on, before you might need that program.

"When you come to a closed door, but you think there is help for your child on the other side, trust God and keep knocking. God is a good God, and He doesn't want you locked out of the resources you need for your child. If you feel you don't have the money, He'll get you the resources. If you feel emotionally drained, He'll provide for your child despite your energy level—your network will drag or carry you along. God will connect you. But you have to be open and honest. Get into a network that might know what to do with the information you are sharing."

Every mother I interviewed said praying God's Word was the strongest source of encouragement, strength, and direction for them and their children during these rough seasons. The second source of strength were people who loved God's Word. Mandy, mom to a depressed teen daughter, had a strong friendship with a friend who had walked that same path. "I would call her for help and advice. I also was able to connect with biblical counselors who have experience in counseling teens. They did not hesitate to encourage me to call to have her professionally evaluated by those experienced in crisis care. God is so good to provide just the right people to help to guide me in the most difficult situations." She went on to explain she learned to err on the side of caution. "Suicide is real…it is so much better to be safe than not." Never feel bad when calling police, psychiatric, or medical professionals.

Lisa encourages parents of prodigals to be wise and use all the resources available to them, Christian and non-Christian alike. If the help aligned with the Word, but wasn't necessarily distributed by a Christian, Lisa still used the advice or resource.

Pray for God's Plan

Take time to evaluate your parenting before God, make any changes you think God is leading you in, and then refuse to guilt or second-guess yourself. One Christian leader, also the mother of a prodigal adult child, gives her perspective: "It would be great to raise kids all over again with the wisdom we have now, but we wouldn't have the energy!" Mom to a prodigal daughter who lived with a man for many years before returning to her faith—and senses— Carol learned regret was counterproductive. "You can look back, but only do so as a means to go forward. By looking back, you might see something about your child that hadn't occurred to you before…use those discoveries to form a plan that can change the course they are on."

Below is a set of questions Norm Wright, a Christian counselor, has his clients ask themselves (ones he too asked, as a parent who had a prodigal child):

- Do you think you were committed enough to your child?
- Do you think you were attentive enough to your child?
- Do you think you were helpful enough with class work?
- Do you think you were loving enough with your child?
- Do you think you spent enough time with your child?
- Do you think you gave your child sufficient discipline?
- Do you think you were firm enough with your child?
- Do you think you allowed enough freedom for your child?
- Do you think you sufficiently encouraged your child?[4]

Taking a good look at your parenting is something all parents should regularly do, not just the parents of prodigals. Life circumstances can force change in families—some good and some not so good. Being constantly aware of the time, energy, and emotion you are putting into your parenting at any given time is a wise use of your time. But an equally wise use of time is to refuse to go on a continual guilt trip. Satan is the accuser. He will make you discouraged, despairing, and depressed, but God's Holy Spirit will point out changes and offer solutions—not just shame, guilt, and depression.

Your expectations of yourself and your child should be realistic. That's why I believe in two key principles of parenting: *the apple doesn't fall far from the tree* and *every child makes his or her own choices in life*. Parents can't take all the credit for how a child turns out—but neither can they take all the blame. There comes a time in every person's life when he or she must take responsibility and quit blaming their parents.

Training Up a Child

An often quoted verse on parenting is Proverbs 22:6, which says: "Train up a child in the way he should go: and when he is old, he will not depart from it" (KJV).

Some people quote this verse as some kind of inalienable right. Like we can tell God, "You owe me! I trained up my child, now give me a godly, productive, successful kid!"

But that's not what it means. Norm Wright explains in his book *Loving a Prodigal,* "The proverbs were never intended to be absolute promises from God. Instead, they are probabilities of things likely to occur. The primary author of Proverbs was Solomon, the wisest man on earth at that time. His purpose was to convey his divinely inspired observations on the way human nature and God's universe work. He was saying that a given set of circumstances can generally be expected to produce a certain set of consequences."[5]

The Hebrew translation of this verse would include a reference to "in the way he should go" to reflect that a parent would consider the age, stage of development, and personality of a child. The Amplified version says, "In keeping with his individual gift or bent." *The Message* says, "Point your kids in the right direction—when they're old they won't be lost."

Dr. Gleason Archer sets up realistic parental expectations. Parenting means, "impressing on them that they are very important persons in their own right because they are loved by God and because He has a wonderful and perfect plan for their lives. Parents who have faithfully followed these principles and practices in rearing their children may safely entrust them as adults to the keeping and guidance of God and feel no sense of personal guilt if a child later veers off course. They have done their best before God. The rest is up to each child himself."[6]

Demonstrate Love When and Where You Can

Rachel, who had an out-of-control pastor's son on the streets, recommends "love them unconditionally regardless of what you see. But you can't do that on your own. Only God can drop that kind of love into your heart. Demonstrate that love with hugs and a kind word or touch." Teresa, a new believer in our own congregation, was concerned for her adult daughter who was moving in with her fiancé months prior to the wedding. Teresa was confused on how much to be involved in the wedding plans since she wasn't in favor of the choice to cohabitate. I prayed with her for wisdom and then said, "Be sure you don't burn any bridge you might want her to walk back over to reach you or Jesus." She decided that she would do only that which she would have done if her daughter had made a healthier choice. Within a year after the wedding, her daughter and son-in-law were active in a church where they have recommitted their lives to Christ and are now serving.

Look for areas your son or daughter *are* doing right and compliment them there. Maybe they are rising in their career or have a unique talent or skill. Treat them at least as well as you would your non-Christian friends! Look for common ground—or create some. Ask them to join you for golf or cooking lessons or some other neutral activity. Give them opportunities to spend time with you and other godly people outside of church.

Set Boundaries, Not Blockades

Renee advises, "Don't try to make life easier—she won't be more cooperative." My friend Debi shared a unique idea to motivate teens and young adults to stay on track. It works great to turn a heart that is "thinking" about rebelling. "When the kids were young and the funds were low, we heard of a pastor in like circumstances. He had a young teenage son who wanted a guitar—more than anything! Even then the guitar cost $600, a sum beyond what the father felt he could afford. Late one night the father received a call from a couple in the church. It seemed their son had gotten into trouble. Could the pastor come down to the police station with them? It was much later by the time the parents were able to bail their son out of jail. As the pastor watched the parents lay down a hefty sum to be able to bring their son home, he couldn't help but think of the guitar his own son wanted.

"The next day father and son made a trip to the music store, and the guitar was purchased. As the pastor gave the guitar to his son, he let him know how thankful he was that he was making wise choices in his life. So the guitar was bought with his 'bail money.' There was a clear boundary— the bail's spent, so if you get in trouble, you're on your own!"

Carol says, "As a parent, even our anger is out of love. When we want to go to the extremes of either disowning him or her to fixing everything, it is because we love them so much *we* can't handle the pain and disappointment. My kids knew I would be supportive when they really wanted to get their act together, but I would not help them continue destructive behavior. They knew God had forgiven everything, so there is nothing that is unforgivable…but you have to want to be forgiven to receive the benefits of forgiveness."

Jasmine says, "Do not be too fast in giving advice. It is so much better to get to the point when *they* come and talk to *you.* If you don't offer the advice first and furiously, they will eventually ask your opinion."

Turmoil in the home is something you can tire of, or even resent, but one mom of a prodigal sees it as a silver lining, "Be grateful that your children are in your home where you can see and hear what is going on in their lives. That way you can observe their behavior and friends and know exactly how to pray and for whom to pray!"

Moms of returned prodigals offer this advice:

- Ask God to help you forgive your child—to help you with your hurt and disappointment in your child. Ask Him to help you see your child through His eyes so you can love your child unconditionally, just as He loves and forgives us.
- Ask God to give you a strong sense of discernment and open opportunities to talk with your children.
- I gained strength from Evelyn Christiansen's *What Happens When We Pray for Our Families*, particularly the releasing prayers. I was able to stop praying protective prayers only and give up the fight to have my own human will over God's divine will. He removed the road blocks I had put up.

Jordan and most of the other prodigals written about in this chapter have returned to a healthy productive lifestyle— and to their faith and family. Most of them cite their parents' unconditional and persistent love as a major factor. Most moms cite prayer as the key. Jordan told me, "There was nothing anyone could have told me that could or would have helped. I knew my choices were wrong. Only God through His Holy Spirit could have turned me back—and He did."

There Is Hope

Life for Dan was a party from the minute he was born. A handsome twin, he and his brother, Dave, garnered attention wherever they went. Dan was spiritually sensitive to God as a child, asking his parents when he could be baptized. The twins, avid skateboarders, dreamed of one day owning their own skate shop. After high school, Dan headed to Santa Rosa to attend college, and Dave soon joined him. The two immersed themselves into the skating party scene. They drifted from God and entered into a business partnership with a nonbelieving skater and took their college money and opened a skate shop. Mom came to visit them and her heart was grieved. The boys had visible signs of rebellion (pierced eyebrows and tongues), but her deeper grief wasn't the outward appearance but how far they had drifted from God and into the partying lifestyle. Even so, God encouraged her with, "Don't look at their appearance, look at their hearts. Their appearance has changed, but their hearts are still Mine. Watch Me work."

Their party lifestyle continued to escalate, causing their business profits to diminish. Things became so tight the brothers lost their apartment and had to move into the skate shop. Finally, one Sunday morning, Dave called home. Hung over from partying the night before, dawn brought with it a moment of clarity. "Mom, the way I've been living is not right. Can I come home?" At semester's end Dave was home.

Dan was not in this same place. Dan did not come home for spring break. One night, a call came from the hospital. Dan and a friend had been skating and were badly injured.

Emergency surgery was performed and a plate and five pins were placed in his ankle. He withdrew from school and stayed with his parents. Away from friends and skating, Dan plunged into a depression.

However, the depression lifted day after day as he experienced the love of God as expressed by his parents. When he could walk again, he took a job managing a local skate shop. God and a godly lifestyle were now what he wanted. He began reaching out to the young skaters who came into the shop. He began hosting a dinner each week where skaters ages 8 to 22 attend. Dan speaks and shares his story and the story of the love of God each week, then the group skates. Any given Monday night Dan will minister to 30–70 skaters. God has prospered him financially, and he bought the skate shop and renamed it *One Way Board Shop*.

◆ ◆ ◆

A PLAN FOR THE PRODIGAL

Get Emergency Help. Some cases, like trouble with the law, a suicide attempt, expulsion from school, or a teen pregnancy, need immediate care. If your son or daughter suffered physical trauma, you'd take them to an emergency room, right? In the same way, most families in crisis need a short-term plan to deal with the issues at hand. A qualified pastor, Christian counselor, or youth leader might be a good first phone call. They will most likely know referrals for your other needs (legal aid, emotional help, schooling, and homes for teens in trouble).

Create a Longer Term Plan That Addresses These Needs:

- ◆ *Help for You and Your Spouse.* If parents feel supported, understood, and strengthened, they make better choices with and for their prodigal. Seek to be a united front and try to stay unified. The prodigal may try to use guilt or manipulation to get one of you to cave in and endorse or subsidize their unhealthy behavior. Use your time in the counseling office to create a unified plan that you both feel you can realistically carry out.

♦ *Help for Your Prodigal.* If they are not willing, use this time to investigate options for when they do become willing. But if they are willing:

—*Go for Something over Nothing.* This means that even if they won't repent, or even acknowledge, that their choices are wrong or unhealthy, ask if they are willing to meet with a pastor, a counselor, or a trusted friend—someone who might break through to them or at least be a part of their team when they do decide to come around.

—*Try to Keep Contact.* It is hard to help if you don't know how to reach them. This isn't always possible, but at least keep your same phone number, email, and home in case they want to contact you. (If this goes on for years, your support team will be a good sounding board for you should you sense the need to move or relocate your family.)

—*Find Something Positive to Build On.* Look for something they *are* doing right. It might take prayer and creativity to discern something, but look for one positive thing and start building on it to rebuild relationship. Oftentimes, this is the cord they use to pull themselves back into God's and your good graces.

It gives them a foundation, something firm to stand on when everything in their life seems unstable.

—*Decide What to Say and Who Needs to Know About the Choices of Your Prodigal.* Decide ahead of time how you will handle questions and unsolicited advice.

—*Stabilize Your Family.* Get a plan together to provide the best care and help for the children who remain in your home and are not prodigals. If you spend all your time on the prodigal, then the other children will feel neglected, and you may end up with a repeat performance. Look for ways to bless and encourage the prodigal's siblings. Try to "normalize" family life as best as you can.

9

THE TREASURE OF TRUST

Transferring the Treasure to Your Teen

If you honor God, God will honor you. That is a phrase my children have heard over and over and over again since they were small. The Bible is full of these examples.

Moses refused to be called Pharaoh's son and instead chose to identify himself with the people of God. After a short stint at the backside of a desert shepherding sheep, he led his people out of captivity and now lives in history.

Daniel refused the king's food and instead chose to eat according to God's laws. Daniel also refused to bow to an idol and was thrown in a lions' den, only to be miraculously saved and elevated by God to leadership of the world's most powerful nation of the time.

Shadrach, Meshach, and Abednego refused to bow and worship the king because they worshiped God. They were thrown into a fiery furnace and saved from it. They were visited there by the Angel of God, which many theologians believe to be Jesus Christ.

God told Samuel to anoint a boy as king, and when Samuel questioned God, He said, "Man looks at the outward appearance, but the LORD looks at the heart" (1 Samuel 16:7). David, a shepherd known as a man after God's own heart, became king of Israel.

Consider theses verses:

> No good thing does He withhold from those who walk uprightly (Psalm 84:11 NASB).
>
> My shield is God Most High, who saves the upright in heart (Psalm 7:10).
>
> Blessed is the man who fears the LORD, who finds great delight in His commands. His children will be mighty in the land; the generation of the upright will be blessed (Psalm 112:1,2).
>
> In my integrity you uphold me and set me in your presence forever (Psalm 41:12).
>
> Righteousness guards the man of integrity (Proverbs 13:6).
>
> Trust in the LORD with all your heart and lean not on your own understanding; in all your ways acknowledge him, and he will make your paths straight (Proverbs 3:5,6).
>
> His master replied, "Well done, good and faithful servant! You have been faithful with a few things; I will put you in charge of many things. Come and share your master's happiness!" (Matthew 25:23).

If my kids didn't get anything else from me during their growing up years, I pray they got this sweeping principle: *Those who honor God, God honors.* All it takes is a humble heart. First Peter 5:6 explains, "Humble yourselves, therefore, under God's mighty hand, that he may lift you up in due time."

"Teen" Means Transition

Bill and I believe a person's basic character is set by the age of 12. You might be able to do a little training and teaching in the junior high years, but it is very difficult to correct character flaws after sixth grade and even harder in high school. Junior highers are said to have the ability to learn volumes of information; however, their moral character is pretty much in place. Yes, it is always possible for God to do an amazing, transforming work in any person's life at any age, but it is just that: Work, and a work that God has to orchestrate and implement.

If you have parented well before age 13, the teen years will be an exciting delight as you watch the fruit of your labors unfold before your very eyes. You have most likely picked up by now a couple of key parental guidelines Bill and I strove to place in our children early:

- ◆ Integrity is not an option. A good name is the best asset you have.
- ◆ Servant hearts will be rewarded. People respond to servant leadership.
- ◆ Never expect others to do what you are unwilling to do.
- ◆ You can't please everyone, so strive to please God. If you please Him, you will most likely also be pleasing those who are godly.
- ◆ A positive attitude won't get you everything, but it will get you a whole lot more than a negative attitude will.

◆ Speak with a respectful attitude. You don't have to agree with me, but you do have to honor me as your parent.

The most important change that needs to happen as a child enters the teen years is a change in parenting styles. When your child was a baby on through elementary school, you set the boundaries, and you decided the rules, schedules, and priorities. However, now that your child is a teen, your job as a parent has changed. Your role now is to systematically, little by little, give all the responsibility for the teen's life to the teen so that by the time they are an adult, they are fully responsible for their own life.

Bill and I often hear parents complain that their 30-year-old still lives at home, or that their young adult daughter keeps dating losers, or that their son can't keep a job. Many times you can trace these kinds of adult stresses back to a lack of their parents' ability to hand the reins over to the child.

If you keep being a directive parent (a benevolent dictator), then in the teen years your son or daughter will feel that they have to wrestle the reins of their life away from you. If you are fortunate, it will come in the form of a teen speaking out. But this isn't always done in a very respectful manner. If you have consistently dictated to them, they may not feel that they will be heard, so they may yell or say ugly things to try to get your attention. Other times it will come in direct acts of rebellion. They just will not do as you have asked. However, the most dangerous form is manipulation and lying. This is when the teen tells you what you want to hear, then does just the opposite when you are not around. This is the most dangerous because it can go undetected for months, sometimes even years, if your child is a good liar.

In our diligence to encourage children toward excellence, we sometimes unknowingly (or knowingly) replace inner conscience and conviction with outer rules and legalism, and this is a danger! Teens are put in a double bind. They don't want to hurt their parents, but they want to somehow fit in. Some teens choose passive-aggressive behaviors of acting one way at home and church, and then looking for an escape valve. Your daughter might walk out the door in a floral mid-calf dress, but has a miniskirt in her purse. Your son might say "Yes, sir," and "Yes, ma'am," then walk right out and do 180 degrees the opposite.

The other extreme is when parents abdicate their duties during the teen years. Some parents expect their 14-year-olds to find all their own rides to and from school, sports, and activities, work to pay for all their own needs, and maybe to help out the family too. Some teens feel that they are not only parenting themselves, but they are parenting their siblings and often their own parents as well.

In these instances, one of three things happens. The teen takes it in stride and decides that their family will never function this way. The second response is one of delayed rebellion. The teen is responsible through young adulthood until maybe their younger siblings are out of the home. Then they want to experience all the fun they missed. This can be dangerous because at this point they could be married or even have children of their own. Most of the time, however, the teen follows their parents' example and refuses to grow up too. This is why you see alcoholism, drug use, and teen pregnancy repeat generation after generation. Neither of the last two make intellectual sense, but most people would rather have the familiar pain instead of unfamiliar change. However, the parents reading this book will not likely be the ones who dump their duties as a parent but rather ones who may err out of good intentions and rein their kids in so tightly that the first hint of freedom they get, they will run for everything that has been labeled as bad.

I have had several friends who grew up on the mission field. One of them relayed the story to me of her best friend. Both girls had parents who were missionaries, but my friend's parents gave her room to grow. She had elbowroom to express her opinions as long as she did it respectfully, and she was asked by her parents to think through her own decisions. Her friend, however, was not allowed to ever disagree with her parents. She was not allowed to try makeup, fashion from the States, or ever be alone with a boy for any reason. She wasn't allowed to think independently. When she went away to Bible college, her parents were shocked to discover she was on probation because she hadn't gone to class, was living off campus with a divorced man who was 15 years her senior, and was pregnant. "How could this happen to our perfect little girl?"

It happened because she was never given responsibility for her own life. She had never thought through her own value system. These kids can easily become prey to the strongest, most charismatic person around them even if that person has a value system opposing the way the child was raised—and sometimes BECAUSE their value system is exactly the opposite of mom and dad's.

Instead of dictating behavior and forcing your will on your teen, think out how you will methodically hand over bit by bit the pieces of their lives. At the end of this chapter you will find several worksheets (contracts) you can give to your teen. This is one way of handling the major areas of responsibility you will need to transfer. These, accompanied with the Learner and Leader contracts, should work to release your teen slowly and carefully into the adult world.

These contracts have their roots in our years in youth ministry. We found our teens needed a tool to give their parents confidence, and the parents needed a tool to help structure the release of responsibility with confidence. We tried to encourage parents to let the teen fight against themselves to set up their own value system rather than fight against mom and dad. If you are a dictator, then a teen may feel the right to rebel simply to express his or her opinions. Teens will often talk out loud, testing their value system.

Teens might say outrageous things like, "What's wrong with sex outside marriage?" "What's the big deal about drinking?" "I'm not sure I believe in God anymore." These statements can shake a parent to the core, so it is little surprising that many parents keep tightening the reins. Unfortunately, tighter reins usually create more outrageous statements, then outrageous behavior.

However, you might allow the teen to think through the major areas of his or her life (relationships, driving, working, education, social commitments, and his or her faith) and then set up the structure, boundaries, AND their own consequences if they violate their own values. You are no longer seen as the bad guy. You simply enforce the consequences the teen has chosen.

This frightens some parents. Many think teens will choose "light sentences," but we have actually experienced the opposite. If you begin when a child is a preteen to involve them in choosing their own punishment, they actually are harder on themselves than you might be.

Let's follow an example through. When our kids are growing up, we give information about sex and relationships on a need-to-know basis. We have three major "talks" with them, and many other mini discussions. When they are early elementary or before (if mom is pregnant), they find out the basics of where babies come from. Then when they are about 9-10, I explain menstruation and how to treat a girl.

This talk comes just before we think any of their friends who are girls might begin menses, so if anything happens to one of their classmates while at school, they are able to handle the situation like a gentleman. Then once in junior high (about sixth grade), Bill takes them out for the talk on handling their own changing bodies, lust, wet dreams, masturbation, and so on. Then the summer before high school, Bill again takes each son and gives them some pointers on how to choose a woman well and how to recognize and avoid high-maintenance women. Both of us join in for a session on why we recommend group dating in high school, and then we assign several books to be read each year in order to gain the next set of privileges. Our children have grown up hearing our story of romance.

Bill and I both came from homes where the marriage wasn't strong or very healthy. My own parents eventually divorced. My mother came to fear for our very lives because of the violent effect alcohol had on my father. Bill and I wanted to do love God's way. We decided to wait until he proposed before we kissed because prior to our rededication to Christ, we'd both been in relationships where the other person we were dating wanted more sexually than we wanted to give and we had felt pressure. We had maintained our virginity in high school but we both knew we were wired hot, so the sexual drive was not something to be taken lightly or a game to be played.

The day Bill bent on one knee, sang me a song he had written, and proposed was the day we first kissed. We have had, to date, 21 very happy and sexually fulfilling years together.

When our children are in junior high, we begin to look at the Relationship Contract worksheet:

Describe the traits of the person you would someday like to marry. List verses you believe reflect whom God would want your son or daughter to someday marry—you do marry whom you date!

Now tell us how you will know if the person you would like to date has those traits. For example, the way a student treats his or her own parents and family rules shows they do or do not respect boundaries. Your child might say they want to marry a Christian, but encourage them to write a more specific description like: "A Christian with an active growing faith that would be reflected in church/youth group attendance, service, and a personal devotional time daily."

What is your dating philosophy? (We recommend reading 2-3 books out of the following: *I Kissed Dating Goodbye, I Gave Dating a Chance, 10 Commandments on Dating,* or *Decide in Two Dates or Less.* See your local bookstore.) Answers would range from courtship only, dating in stages, and everything in between! The key is that both the kids and parents pray through and agree on the philosophy AHEAD of time. It is important to develop open dialogue on this topic because the details of the Relationship Contract may evolve over time.

What is the definition of a date? Ours is any prearranged time between two people.

How will I know you are responsible enough to:

- ◆ Group date?
- ◆ Double date?
- ◆ Single date?

What kinds of dates will you go on at what age? A discussion of proms and other special activities should be included.

188 THE TREASURE INSIDE YOUR CHILD

Write a list of at least 10 active dates. Active dates are those that foster discussion and keep the daters steering clear of temptation. Passive dates like movies, videos, and "hanging out" are setups for a sexual fall.

What are God's physical standards for my relationships at what stage? We draw a line with a continuum on it starting with holding hands and ending with sexual intercourse, then we have our sons look up a variety of Bible verses and mark the chart with a line for casual relationships, serious dating headed to courtship, engagement, and marriage only.

Who will pay for dates? How will they be paid for? We don't underwrite our kids' social lives except for youth group events.

Who are two people—one best friend, one adult other than my parents—whom I can give this contract to so they will hold me accountable? These people will help you guide and guard your precious children as they begin exploring relationships with the opposite sex.

What are the consequences if I break my contract? Have them list consequences for first, second, and third offenses. This is imperative because then they are now the "heavy" and you will only enforce what they have already set in place as their own consequence.

Then add any family traditions you have in this area. For example, we want to meet anyone who our sons are interested in possibly dating. No one of the opposite sex is allowed in our sons' rooms or over when we are not home. Also, when our sons think they are ready to solo date, they must meet with the parents of the girl and explain their standards and ask for permission to date their daughter. You might have your own traditions.

Then each of you will sign and date the document. We encourage you to begin discussion of these issues early, all during the preteen years (8-12) and write the Relationship Contract early. The longer you wait to have your student write the contract, the more likely conflict will occur, but it is never too late. Even as a son or daughter sets off for college, it is still important to communicate on these issues. If you are contributing financially to their education, you have the right to not pay for sinful lifestyle choices. If your college student wants to live with a partner, you can cut off their college funds. We've found the more we talk out these issues ahead of time, the less likely any conflict will occur. The best way to guarantee your children will have a happy marriage is to protect them from poor relationship choices as a teen and young adult, and the Relationship Contract is one tool to help your son or daughter decide before God that they too want healthy, happy relationships and will make choices to ensure that can happen.

Train, Then Transfer

As our kids have grown, we have tried to train all along the way. On the Learner and Leader chore chart, it might have said, "Clean your room," but I knew my version of clean and a nine-year-old's would be very different, so early on I made 3 x 5 cards and a checklist they could run down so they would know what I meant by a clean room. For example:

- ◆ Fold clothes and put them away
- ◆ Dust shelves, headboard, desk, and tables
- ◆ Put toys in right bins
- ◆ Organize papers and books so I could find something if you sent me to your room to find it

I want to set my kids up for success. That's why we have the running parenting philosophy of *you can make your own decision as soon as I know you are prepared to make the right decision.* This is where the transfer begins.

Pros and Cons

As the kids hit eight, nine, ten and eleven, we would sit down with them when any kind of major decision came and say: "We need to make a decision. Let's make a list of pros and cons for each option and then pray and see how God leads us." We didn't do this for every decision in the children's elementary years, just in strategic times when we thought the situation was a good setup for learning decision-making skills.

Here is an example: Zach was on an all-star baseball team that had a Sunday game when he was nine. Bill and I sat down with him and we made a list.

Pros

- He would keep his commitment to the team.
- He could go to the 8:30 service before the 11:30 game.
- He could take Jesus with him, and even offer to pray before the game.
- It is a play-off game. If he is missing, they might lose, and he might have made the difference.
- A parent has already volunteered to pick him up at church and take him so Mom and Dad won't have to miss their responsibilities.
- Mom and Dad can come and see the last half of the game and have lunch there with Brock and Caleb and pick up Zach.

◆ The non-Christians might see his missing the game as a sign of his religion being legalistic with no flexibility.

Cons

◆ Some might see this as putting baseball over God.

◆ Mom and Dad might get caught after church and only make the last inning or so.

◆ Everyone only gets fast food and not a nice Sunday lunch.

◆ Zach will miss children's church (but not Sunday school).

◆ Mom and Dad can't drive him there. Are Zach and Mom and Dad comfortable with the person who volunteered?

Zach decided that this time, because he could still go to church at 8:30 and because he was strategic for a win in a play-off, he would go. We felt comfortable with the parent who volunteered, and our family had been praying theirs would come to faith in Christ and begin attending church. We talked at length and prayed together as a family over who should be offended, a non-Christian whom you hope you can lead to Jesus or Christians who are already going to heaven. We talked about gray areas, like playing ball on a Sunday. We contrasted Eric Liddell's refusal to run on a Sunday in the Olympics (Zach had seen the movie *Chariots of Fire*) with today's Christian athletes who play on Sunday but use their professional platform as a great way to share the gospel to thousands every year.

In the end, Zach decided God wanted him to go and be there for the team. He cited two main factors: "I can still attend church first service, and because it is a play-off, this game has a higher value than a regular game to my team. I feel I shouldn't let them down."

However, the next fall, Zach made a different choice when a game that was scheduled for Sunday at 1:00 was moved to 10:30. It was a regular game, it was winter ball (so no standings were taken), and he'd have to miss both worship services. Zach called his coach and said, "Coach, Jesus is more important to me than baseball. Because the game got moved to a time when my family attends church and there are no other options for me to attend at a different time, I will miss this week's game. Could you tell the league board that it would be helpful if they kept their word? I signed up because they said all games would be on Sunday after 1:00 and this one isn't, so that means all of us kids have to make a choice to skip church if our families go to church. I don't think that is right. Sorry, Coach. I'll pray you still win." That season, two more games were moved and Zach missed both of them to attend church. He said it was a matter of principle. The games were supposed to be at 1:00 and they changed them. After that season, Zach made a decision to never sign up for a league in any sport that played only Sunday games.

Had we laid down the law and just imposed our decision, our son might have rebelled because he didn't understand, and he would have missed out on the foundation that was laid for future decisions.

Tell Me Why I Should Say "Yes!"

We move from the powwow as a team over a pro/con list to the next step as our kids hit the eighth grade/freshman year in school. The decision on where they will attend school in high school is one of the last powwows we have in eighth grade, then we try to move, as often as possible, to the "tell me why I should say yes" model. For example, Brock had a new friend from football call and ask if he could spend the night and then go to Disneyland the next day with the friend's grandparents. Brock looked up at us from the phone and asked if he could go. We could have made an instant decision, Bill and I, but instead we said, "Brock, get as much information as possible and tell him you will call him back after you talk to your parents."

Brock hung up the phone and we said, "Tell us why we should say yes."

Because Brock had been used to doing the pro/con lists with us for several years now, he created his own on a piece of paper. Then he wrote down questions he knew we'd ask and the answers to them.

Pro

◆ I love Disneyland and haven't gone for a while.
◆ I have my own money I can use if Mom and Dad say I have to use it.
◆ Mom knows James because she takes him home everyday from football.
◆ Mom likes James.
◆ James' grandparents will be driving.
◆ I don't have any commitments on Saturday.
◆ I can get my chores done on Thursday that I would normally do on Saturday.
◆ I have been responsible in handling my way to and from school. I always call if there is a problem. I know how to ask for help, directions, and how to avoid weirdos and strangers. I can handle navigating Disneyland even if James and I are on our own.

Cons
- ◆ Mom and Dad haven't met James' grandparents.
- ◆ I don't know if they will be with us or if they will let us be on our own at Disneyland.

Brock then got back on the phone and called James. "Hey, I just need a little more information for my parents. I know this might sound weird, but my parents don't know your grandparents. Are they good drivers? You know, they don't drink and drive or anything like that, do they? Yeah, I didn't think so since your parents are letting you go with them, but my mom's dad was an alcoholic, so that stuff is important to her. Oh, and will we be with them all day or on our own? Yeah, I kind of thought we'd be on our own. We'll probably run from ride to ride to get the most in. I guess I can't see them wanting to run, huh?"

I smiled at Brock's candor and at the risk he was taking. Brock knew that I knew that because James' parents had beer in their own refrigerator (he had told me that after spending the night there), that I would want to know about the drinking and driving thing.

We ran down one last checklist of emergency scenarios: "What if you get separated from James?"

"James and I will have a emergency meeting place where we can meet each other or his grandparents if we get separated."

"Do you have Dad's cell number memorized?" He reeled it off.

"What if you get up there and James was wrong and his grandparents have had alcohol with dinner?" He didn't like this question. He knew that if he said he wouldn't ride with them, then James would be offended. But he knew this was a deal breaker with us, and if he caved in and said he'd get in the car we'd say no. He stood silent for a moment.

"Brock, this will not be the first time you will have to make this choice."

Then Bill and I each shared times we had and had not made the right choice in this area.

Brock finally said, "If I were a real friend, I wouldn't want James to ride in the car either if his grandparents were drinking. I guess I'd call home and talk over the decision with you two if that really did happen."

"Good answer. Call James and say yes and get the details—if we need to drop you off, what time, and where."

The Treasure of Trust

Trust begets trust. Help your children build trust with you as they become teens. Surround your teen with many voices that echo the whisper of the Holy Spirit. The treasure of trust is complete when you no longer lead your child— but God does.

Don't Overreact. One way to build trust so your teen will share information necessary for you to release more responsibility is not to overreact. Trust can be hard for parents who love their kids. Take a deep breath if you need to before discussing a situation you may be concerned about.

Remember to Thank Your Teen for a Trustworthy Act. Brock asked at the dinner table, "Mom, Dad, Friday night Brandon wants a couple of us to spend the night. And I'll tell you why you should say yes. Brandon's mom will be there. We just want to hang out and maybe watch some movies. Brandon's on the football team; Mom knows him. I don't know if you have met his mom, but when Dad drops me off, he could meet her. Mom, since you have to fly out this weekend, I could take your car so if anything happened that I knew you wouldn't approve of, I could drive myself home. But then you would have to talk to Brandon's mom on the phone ahead of time, Dad. I would still be home early enough Saturday to do all my work and homework. You know everyone who is invited" (and he listed them off. They were all kids we knew, and about half were strong Christian kids like our son).

Bill said, "Since I'm the one home this weekend, I'll call Brandon's mom, and if I like the answers I get, then you can go." Bill called and everything seemed to be on the up-and-up. Bill did find out that Brandon's mom was a single mom, so he added a stipulation, "If any adults there are acting in a manner your mom and I would not approve of, then I want you to come home." (We've had to start adding this one in because so many of the boys' friends have parents who have sex outside of marriage, drink, watch movies we don't approve, etc. We count on the grown-ups to be grown up.) Brock agreed.

After Brock had been gone about an hour and a half, Bill got a call. "Dad, can you come get David? My license won't let me drive with anyone else in the car, and some seniors showed up with a bunch of alcohol and we want to leave. Can he come to our house and spend the night?"

"Sure. But where's Brandon's mom?"

"She's here. But she's in her room, and all she does is yell at Brandon to 'get those kids with that booze out of here.' Dad, Brandon keeps trying but they won't go. We *all* asked them and they won't leave."

Bill sensed the severity of the situation. He knew that either the seniors were just going to stay and be allowed to drink or a fight could ensue or the police would be called. All were negative options.

"Yes, I'll come right now. Meet me outside with all your stuff immediately—"

"Dad, wait. Rodney's here too. He and a couple of the others want to leave and Rodney said he'd drop off David at our place."

We knew Rodney. He was a Christian kid from a good family who lived a few blocks from us.

"Ok, and if you want all of the kids to come over, Brock, they are welcome."

"Thanks, Dad."

It turned out several stayed, not wanting to abandon Brandon. But several came and hung out at our home. Bill and I were proud of Brock, and Bill complimented all the guys on making a right choice.

For the next few months, every time Brock would ask permission for a privilege, he'd run down the answers to the questions and I'd say yes and add, "I can easily say yes because you've been so trustworthy. You have a good head on your shoulders."

We are constantly told by other adults what a responsible, mature son we have, which we then relay to Brock. We have told him that trust builds trust, but Brock has also experienced this past year that trust bring privileges from other people, like great letters of recommendation, opportunities to go places with people, and do things that kids who are a problem don't get to do. Brock is getting to see, without us saying it, *those who honor God, God honors.*

Relationship Contract

Traits of the person I'd someday like to marry: Internal traits are best (like honest), not external (like "cute"):

How will I know the person has those traits? (What evidence am I looking for?)

What is my definition of a "date"?

What is my dating "philosophy"? (date in high school? college? only for courtship?)

How will your parents know you are responsible enough to:

group date?

double date?

single date?

What age is it ok to go on what kind of dates? (For example: When can you go to prom? bowling? etc.)

List 10 "active" dates (like mini golf or bike riding):

As you look to God's Word, what physical standards will you keep? (For example, no sex before marriage is a command in the Bible.) Draw a line at where you will maintain your standards:

hold hands	hugs	a kiss	kisses	make out	petting	fore- play	inter- course/ oral sex

(We recommend you move the line back as far as you need to to maintain a pure heart and mind.)

Who will pay for dates?

Who will I give a copy of this contract to that will hold me accountable besides my parents (youth leader, Christian friend, etc.)?

Are there any family traditions (like parents need to meet a person first before a date, etc.)?

Consequences if I violate my contract:

Offense 1:

Offense 2:

Offense 3:

Signed: _____ (parents)

    _____

    _____ (student)

Date: _____

Driving Contract

Who arranges for permit, classes, tests, etc.? (Some parents think that if you aren't mature enough and motivated enough to arrange for the classes, you aren't ready to drive...)

Who pays for what? (who pays for car? gas? insurance? upkeep? Lots of options! Example: Mom and Dad pay for car with the stipulation that every time it goes to church it is filled with other kids! Or maybe you pay for gas and insurance, they pay for car. Or maybe you get use of family car, or maybe you pay for it all! Driving isn't a right but a privilege.)

Who can be in your car?

Where can you drive and when?

What activities are allowed? (Can you eat and drive? listen to music and drive?)

Who pays for tickets? (What other consequences should there be for tickets? an accident? breaking your contract, etc.?)

Consequence for first infraction:

For second infraction:

For third infraction:

Signed: _____ (parents)

_____

_____ (student)

Date: _____

Work Contract

Where can I work? (how far from home? what kinds of jobs?)

How will I get there?

How many hours a week?

How is the money to be used?

What conditions? (keep a certain GPA, keep up with at-home chores? etc.)

Consequences for violating contract:

First offense:

Second offense:

Third offense:

Signed: _____ (parents)

_____

_____ (student)

Date: _____

Education Contract

(Can use for schooling decisions junior high through college)

What are my educational goals?

Where will I attend school?

Who pays for what?

What conditions? (behaviors, GPA, etc.)

Consequences:

First offense:

Second offense:

Third offense:

Signed: _____ (parents)

_____

_____ (student)

Date: _____

10

GOD MARKS THE SPOT

*Helping Your Child Recognize
and Respond to God's Call*

A key component of parenthood is to pass on the baton of faith and values to the next generation. Parenthood has the goal of helping a child mature into the person God designed. The most productive and fulfilled adults are those who have discovered and are living out God's unique call on their lives. When a person finds his or her passion, they are able to keep going and going and going. Life isn't such drudgery. There is a kind of thrill and adventure because you are a part of God's larger plan of reaching people with the good news of His love.

Help Your Child to Know His or Her Faith and Be Able to Communicate that Faith

Bill and I believe a child should have a platform on which to share Christ by the time they are 13. Adolescence will go smoother for those teens who have something they feel they are competent at, something that makes them feel special, visible, and that they value. But once they have that platform, how can they stand on it and share their faith?

A Little Bit at a Time

The best way to help a child learn how to share his or her faith is to model it by sharing yours. Let your child see and hear you have spiritual conversations. Let them see you serve God. Include them in the prayers you have when praying for those you would like to see come to faith in Christ.

When Brock was about five years old and on his first T-ball team, we prayed for each player on the team and their family. The prayers were simple: "Lord, we pray for Jimmy. Please help us show him and his family Your love. Please reach their hearts and introduce Yourself to them. Please let them come to You."

When Brock was 15, he was the master of ceremonies at the first Banquet of Champions sponsored by the Fellowship of Christian Athletes club he founded. As a part of the banquet, a pro athlete shared the gospel and gave an invitation to receive Christ. Jimmy prayed to accept Christ that night. Though many have come to faith in Christ through the many outreaches Brock and Zach have hosted, Jimmy's decision was extra special because our family had been praying for it for over ten years.

Let Them Help

My friend and the music director at our church, Debe, has helped her children in sharing their faith in all kinds of ways over the years. The first Christmas we lived in San

Diego, I was discipling Debe. We decided we'd invite people to a Christmas party and we'd include everyone in our families in some way. We wanted to share the gospel with our guests. We assigned her daughter Karly, then nine, with the task of directing a Christmas pageant of the Christmas story with the cast of whatever children came, including Brock and Zach, who were six and four, and her younger siblings, including Debe's baby, who would play the baby Jesus!

Karly stepped right up to the plate and created a wonderful drama with amazing costumes. The crowd wasn't very big that night, but little by little over the years, Karly was given more and more responsibility in dramatic presentations both onstage and behind the scenes. The audiences are much bigger now that she directs her own children's theater, Connections. She founded her children's musical theater with the purpose of training children to share their faith through the arts. Her ministry has grown to several groups and a publisher is looking at her creative scripts and choreography.

Party with a Purpose

One of the best ways to train children to share their faith is to entertain evangelistically. There are so many opportunities in a child's life to party with a purpose: Christmas, Easter, before or after children's dramas, during a sports season, or in conjunction with a church event. Let's use a Happy Birthday Jesus Party as an example.

This Christmas party can include the basic party ingredients:

1. Welcome. This is a great entry-level ministry opportunity—even a preschooler can hand out stickers to guests as they enter, or a nametag, or candy cane.

2. Icebreaker or game. Every party needs entertainment. Simple games or crafts for young children, or icebreaker contests for teens, work well to make guests feel at home. This is a great second step for a child to take.

3. A testimony. A one-minute testimony of faith is a great start for a junior higher. This was the testimony Zach gave at his freshman football outreach:

> Many of you know Reggie White as the "Minister of Defense." That's his nickname. He was twice named Defensive Player of the Year and has been selected to the Pro Bowl 12 times! What is Reggie's source of strength? Why is he my favorite player? I can relate to him. When he was 13 years old, he went to church and his pastor was a really cool guy. He liked what he saw in his pastor's life and found out it was Jesus. So he asked Jesus to come into his life then—and a personal relationship with God has been a source of strength for him ever since.
>
> My dad is a pastor, and I saw things in his life I liked too. One Father's Day, I told my parents I wanted to know God. I bowed my head and prayed and asked Jesus to come into my life, and He did. Since then God has been the source of my strength for many things— like trying new sports, meeting new friends, and for talking to you right now.

As Brock entered high school and began having sports outreaches, he adapted his testimony to the audience. He began to grow in his ability to share his faith. Here's a sample of the testimony he gave at his football pizza party:

> What do I have in common with Barry Sanders, John Carney, Mark Brunell, and Deion Sanders? Not

football ability! It's that all these players and myself have a personal relationship with Jesus Christ that gives each of us the strength and focus we need to succeed.

We're freshman now—and I have a challenge. I think we can be the winningest varsity team San Marcos has ever seen. I think we can be our personal best if we have three things: dedication, determination, and desire.

First, dedication. Play as a team. One of the first things I learned from God's playbook, the Bible, was "Do unto others as you would have them do unto you." We will play as a team when we think of the team and not just ourselves.

Second, determination. The Bible says those who know their God can do mighty things, and my favorite verse says I can do all things through Christ who strengthens me. God can help us work hard and not get distracted by things that can ruin our futures—like premarital sex, drugs, drinking, and fighting. God promises to be there for each of us no matter what. Danny Wuerffel is an example of determination. In 1996 he won the Heisman trophy and was named the College Hall of Fame Scholar Athlete. He credits his personal relationship with God as the motivating factor to this accomplishment.

Third, desire. It could be easy for us to say, "We don't have hot uniforms, and we don't have a new stadium." We could see ourselves as second-rate, but God doesn't see us that way. God made us and He thinks we're first-rate—we just need to believe it and act like it! When I was just seven years old, I learned that God's desire was to help me be the best I could be, and I asked Jesus to come into my life and God has been keeping His promise to help me ever since

Super Bowl veteran Eugene Robinson says, "Success is maximizing the opportunities where God has placed me." Today, you're going to hear about some opportunities that will help you maximize your potential and I hope you'll take advantage of them.

4. *The gospel.* The final step is a simple gospel presentation. Following is a sample of the gospel presentation Brock gave:

God has a game plan for your life. That game plan is:

1. God loves you and offers you a wonderful plan for your life.

Jesus said, "I came that they might have life, and might have it abundantly" (John 10:10 NASB). Jesus also said that "God so loved the world, that He gave His only begotten Son, that whoever believes in Him should not perish, but have eternal life (John 3:16 NASB).

What prevents us from knowing God and His game plan?

2. Man is sinful and separated from God. That's why people don't experience God's game plan for life.

The Bible says, "All have sinned and fall short of the glory of God" (Romans 3:23).

None of us, if we stood on a free throw line, would make 100 percent of the shots we take. God knew we were imperfect, so He came up with a plan to reconnect us to Him.

3. Jesus Christ is God's only provision for our imperfection. Through Jesus we can know and experience God's love and plan for our life. "God demonstrates his own love for us in this: While we were still

sinners, Christ died for us" (Romans 5:8). Jesus said, "I am the way and the truth and the life. No one comes to the Father except through me" (John 14:6).

But it's not just enough to know these truths.

4. We must each individually receive Jesus as our Savior and Lord. Then we can know God personally and experience His love and plan for our life.

It's like we need to ask God to be our coach in life. "As many as received Him, to them He gave the right to become children of God, even to those who believe in His name" (John 1:12 NASB). Jesus said, "Behold, I stand at the door and knock; if anyone hears My voice and opens the door, I will come in to him" (Revelation 3:20 NASB).

Asking God to be the coach of my life is the best decision I've ever made, and as we end here I just want to pray out loud a prayer like the one I prayed. As I pray, if you want to make the decision to ask God to coach your life, then you can pray along with me silently.

Jesus, thank You for loving me and offering me a great game plan for my life. I know I am imperfect and that You paid for that imperfection when You died for me on the cross. Please come into my life to be my Savior and Coach. Make me the kind of person You designed me to be. Thanks. Amen.

Pray for Outside Opportunities for Your Child to be Trained to Communicate His or Her Faith

Organizations like Child Evangelism's Good News Clubs, Student Venture, Fellowship of Christian Athletes, Athletes of Good News, Young Life and many other church and parachurch youth groups give this kind of training. As your children join in these groups and step into the opportunities they offer, then more opportunities will be opened up to them. Brock is asked to open our city council in prayer on a regular basis. Zach has been asked to lead Sunday school classes, and Caleb has hosted several Christmas and Easter outreaches for his friends and teammates.

What if your child is older and more shy or reserved? Help them learn to use quieter ways to share the gospel. Have them write the family Christmas letter and ask them to include the gospel somehow in it. Have them create birthday or Christmas cards on the computer with a Scripture verse included in the well wishes. Ask them to play their instrument for the family Christmas gathering, and ask them to play a hymn or carol and then give out cards or gifts with a section of the lyrics attached. Make care packages for the homeless with *God Loves You* stickers on them. Pray, and God will give your entire family ways to share His love.

Help Your Child to Know How to Discern the Will of God and Hear His Call

Really, this entire book is an attempt to understand and recognize the will of God on the life of your child. But as a child gets ready to fly from the nest, the stakes go up. So what are some principles for knowing God's will?

What Is God's Will for Me?

There are only a few statements in the New Testament that clearly say, "This is God's will" or "This pleases God." I believe when we are obeying those statements, then all decisions made while obeying them become God's will. There is freedom in obeying the basic responsibilities God has laid out. Encourage your young adult to ask, am I:

Saved? "This is good, and pleases God our Savior, who wants all men to be saved and to come to knowledge of the truth" (1 Timothy 2:3,4).

Spirit-filled? "Do not get drunk on wine, which leads to debauchery. Instead, be filled with the Spirit" (Ephesians 5:18).

Sanctified? "Therefore, I urge you, brothers, in view of God's mercy, to offer your bodies as living sacrifices, holy and pleasing to God—this is your spiritual act of worship. Do not conform any longer to the pattern of this world, but be transformed by the renewing of your mind. Then you will be able to test and approve what God's will is—his good, pleasing and perfect will" (Romans 12:1,2).

Sexually Pure? "It is God's will that you should be sanctified: that you should avoid sexual immorality" (1 Thessalonians 4:3).

Saying Thanks? "Give thanks in all circumstances, for this is God's will for you in Christ Jesus" (1 Thessalonians 5:18).

Suffering for Right? "So then, those who suffer according to God's will should commit themselves to their faithful Creator and continue to do good" (1 Peter 4:19).

Seeking God? "Blessed are they who keep his statutes and seek him with all their heart" (Psalm 119:2).

What Spiritual Markers Do You Remember?

Often, by looking back, we can see how God has uniquely prepared us for our passion. Your child might have been raised knowing more than one language, or living in another culture, or receiving special training. God is also the master of turning a pain into a platform for ministry. The burning bush was a marker for Moses. He knew that God had spoken to him at a specific period of time and called him to lead his people even when he was hiding in the desert. Moses had other markers too. He was saved when other baby boys were being killed by Pharaoh. As he grew, he had to have asked, "Why me? Why was I saved?" He was educated in Egypt. When God sent him back to Egypt, who in all of Israel would have been better prepared to speak to the ruler but someone raised in the palace?

God places markers—clues—in every life, and as we look for them and help our children see them, we gain wisdom on how to focus our lives. God built the markers into your child's life for a reason. He will direct their path.

Have your young adult complete the following exercises for more insight into their own calling:

> *What are my successes?* Have them list their top five favorite or most meaningful moments of achievement.
>
> *What is my uniqueness?* What does your child do differently or better than average? Os Guinness in *The Call* says we need to replace "We are what we do," with "Do what we are."[1]
>
> *What are my markers?* Have him or her write five to seven sentences about times when he or she gave her life away—was other-focused—and they felt, "Wow! That went well! I think I helped someone!" Then go back over those sentences and look for common threads. Maybe all the people are a certain age or in a certain circumstance. Or maybe the common thread is doing things that help people like research, design, or taking care of things like computers.
>
> *What are my gifts?* There are many spiritual gift tests, but the best way to discern a gift is to try many ways of serving God and then look for the response, outcome, or validation. Often, people that know us

best will compliment us when we are exercising our gifts. Help your young adult by listing compliments others have said about him or her to you. Or go one better: Ask those adults that are most important to your launching teen to speak or write their observations.

Help Your Child by Letting Go

Carol Kuykendall, author of *Give Them Wings*, reminds us that the task of adolescence, "is to separate and gain independence; to pull away and find an answer to the question, 'Who am I, apart from this family?' "[2]

Carol shares a story of the day her teen son came home with an earring in his ear. She was wise enough not to overreact, but instead she asked herself some vital questions, "Retaining total control is not my goal in dealing with an adolescent. My aim is to empower that adolescent by giving him control that enables him to make his own decisions. So I try to clarify the conflict in my mind: Is this an issue about who is in control or about a boy wearing an earring?...Why is this issue bothering me so much? Do I want him to change his appearance for my benefit...or his? Is this my problem or his? Is this issue morally threatening or life threatening?...Am I allowing him to express his opinion?"[3]

This separation is not easy for the parent nor does it feel natural—but it is vital. I can count on one hand the number of times Brock has been in any kind of conflict with me, but mini episodes of "digging his heels in" seemed to be happening with more frequency when he was nearly 17. I suddenly was hearing, "Ok, ok" when I asked him to do something, or an "All right, Mom" with a bit of an attitude when I reminded him of a deadline or responsibility. Genes carry many traits, and one of the unfortunate ones Brock received from me was a propensity for acne. Though not nearly as bad as mine was at his age, I have been concerned for him because I know the long-term effects. Even so, I have been careful not to pass on my feelings about my acne struggles to Brock. I have tried to be rational, helpful, and resourceful in offering him options—not overwrought emotions—in dealing with the issue. He has gone through several medications, doctor appointments, and treatments trying to find one that would work easily into his busy schedule. One night I asked him if he had tried the new medical treatment I had ordered for him.

He exploded. "It's *my* face! I don't know why this is such a big deal for you!" He poured out a torrent of emotion. I thought about using humor, but he didn't seem to be in the mood. I thought about forcing the issue, knowing he might thank me later, but forcing a six-foot football player to wash his face with fancy products didn't seem to even be rational. I thought about ultimatums. I knew I could take his keys (and I even went and got them!). I could keep them until he got into the habit of taking better care of his face, but that seemed like an overreaction.

In the end, I walked up to him and said, "Brock, you know I love you. You know I want the best for you. You know I always prepare you for success; that's why I always trained you in something before I released responsibility to you. I did it with driving, with relationships, with work—this is just another area. You are a gorgeous man, and I know you want to stay that way. I have provided products and doctor's training for you. I now release you to choose well for yourself." I laid his keys and the product down. "Honey, this won't be the last impasse we'll have. You have the major areas of life handled well already, so it is the little things—

the little things that can turn into big things if we don't communicate. So we'll keep the conversation open, ok? You are a terrific son, and I am fortunate to have you in my life." Then he gave me a huge hug, and hung on for a really long time.

"I know, Mom, I love you for helping me succeed."

Those words from my son are about the sweetest words a parent will ever hear. Because our children are so precious to us, we do want them to succeed in life—in the big things and the little things—and fully become everything God designed them to be. Pay close attention to your map (God's Word), hold tightly onto your key (faithful prayer), follow your treasure-hunting Guide (the Holy Spirit), and you will successfully unlock the treasure inside your child.

◆　◆　◆

LONG-DISTANCE LOVING

As your children mature, you will need new ideas to stay emotionally connected to them in a new, more adult friendship role. Here are a few:

- Keep a supply of picture postcards from the hometown area on hand for quick, one-liner messages.
- Clip articles of interest from the newspaper or send the sports section.
- Send a few family photos with captions.
- Send church newsletters.
- Send a tape you've enjoyed. Make a tape.
- Have a little brother or sister draw a picture.
- Write some "Proverbs from Home," starting with Proverbs 32, as the Bible stops at 31. This is a good way to tuck in some advice.[4]

- Email photos, prayers for their day, or have automatic email greetings or thoughts for the day sent from Christian Internet sites that offer these options.

- Send money, stamps, or a gas or phone card tucked in a letter. (They may call to say "Thanks!")

- Invest in a timeshare, cabin, or other recreation activity that you and your young adult children and married children would enjoy with you.

- Send gifts of encouragement and applause. We were newlyweds when my husband graduated from seminary. My mother sent Bill a new white shirt and tie for "all those Sundays ahead."

- Send comfort gifts: Mom would send me Grandma's cookies and candies or brands of products I used growing up, like Avon hand cream to tuck in my purse.

- Care packages: I received a birthday in a box from my mom when I was away at school. I had all the ingredients for a cake, popcorn, candy, streamers, etc. There was always enough for a party in the care packages. Friends in my dorm were always happy to see my mom's packages arrive!

Treasure
Hunt
Journal

*As described in chapter seven, I encourage you
to use this journal to find the treasure in your children
and write down specific prayers for each one.*

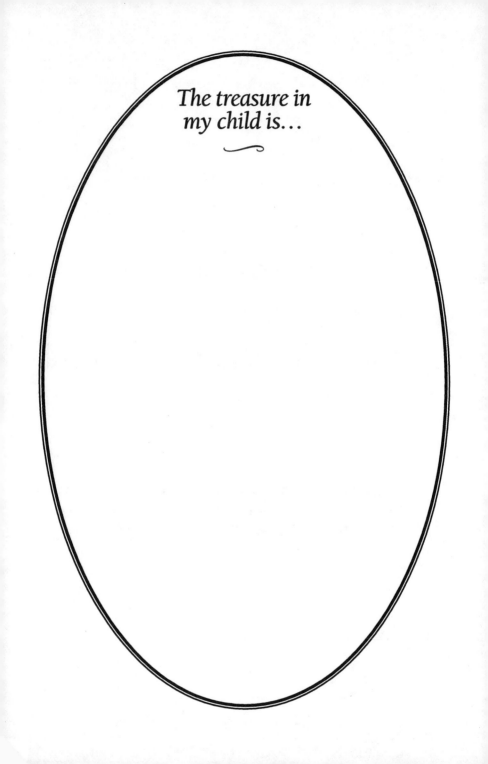

*The treasure in
my child is...*

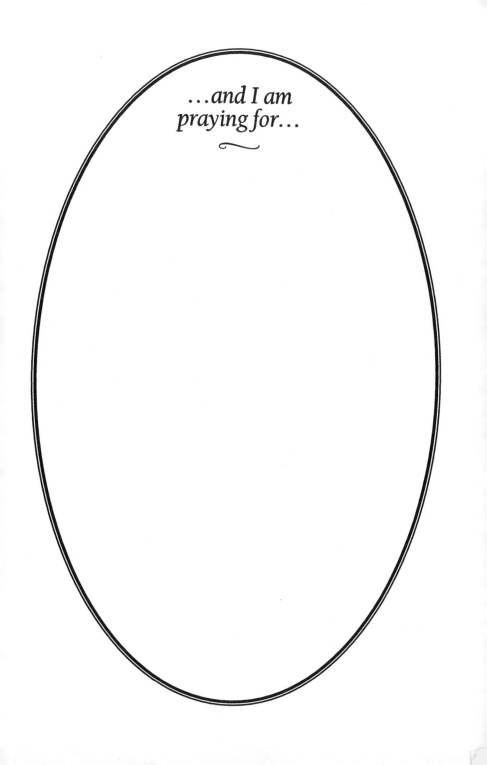

*...and I am
praying for...*

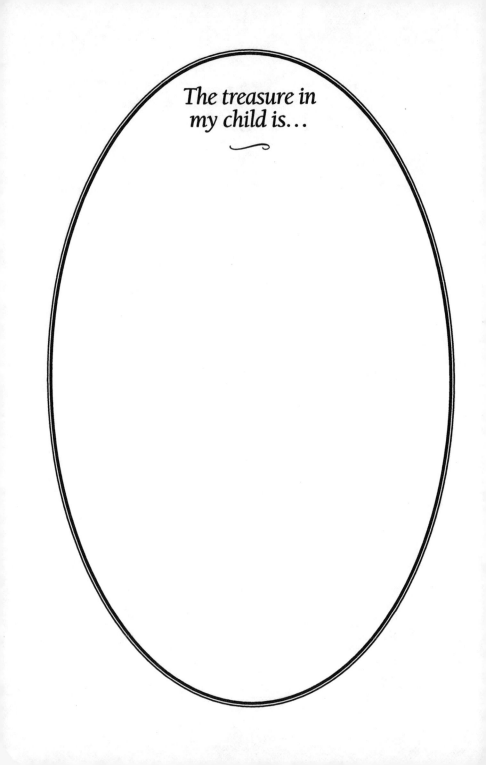

The treasure in
my child is...

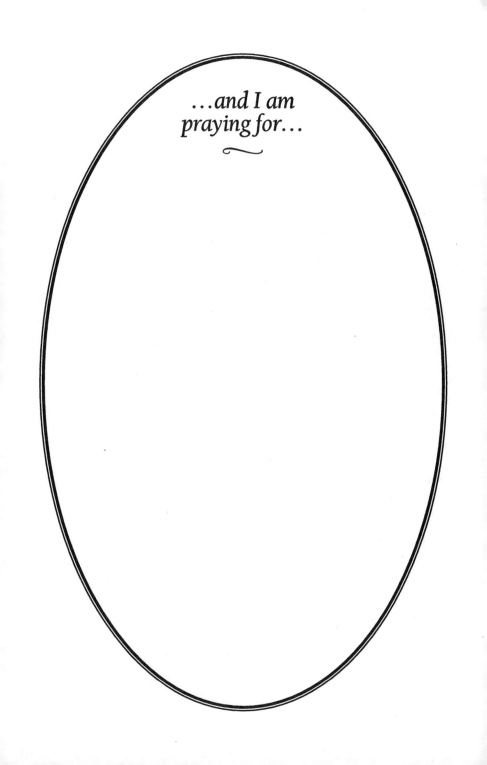

...and I am praying for...

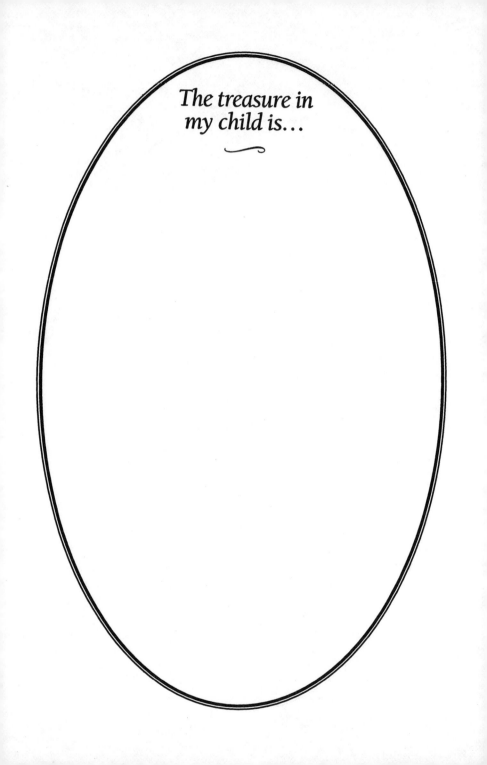

The treasure in
my child is…

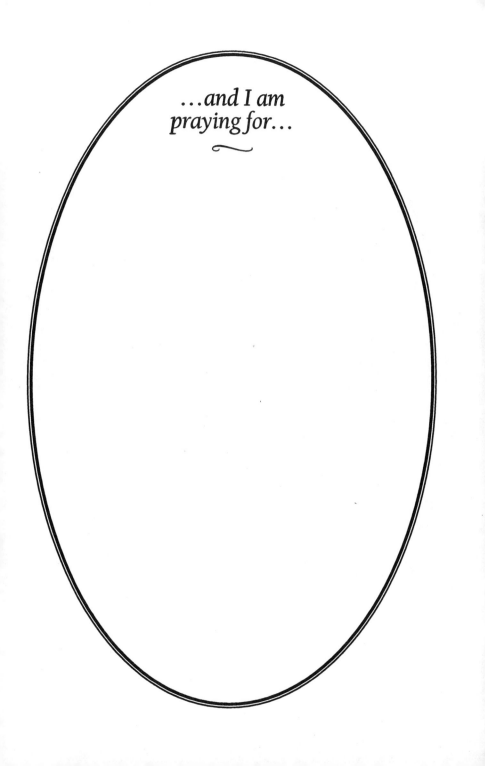

*...and I am
praying for...*

Recommended Resources

Personality:
CLASS
PO Box 66810
Albuquerque, NM 87193
(Offers a very inexpensive personality test)

Christian Financial Concepts
PO 2377
Gainesville, GA 30503
(Offers Career Direct / Life Pathways to help your children decide on major and career)

DISC Test
Personality Insights
PO Box 28592
Atlanta, GA 30358

The Delicate Art of Dancing with Porcupines: Learning to Appreciate the Finer Points of Others
by Bob Phillips
(A resource book on temperaments, behavior styles, and social styles)

Spiritual Gifts Inventory
Church Growth Institute
PO Box 7
Elkton, MD 21922

Books
Celebrate! I Made a Big Decision: Creating a Spiritual Scrapbook with Your Child
by Pam Farrel

The New Birth Order Book
by Kevin Leman

Unlocking Your Child's Learning Potential
by Cheri Fuller

The Way They Learn
by Cynthia Tobias

Organizations
Family Life Today
3900 N. Rodney Parham Rd.
Little Rock, AR 72212

Focus on the Family
Colorado Springs, CO 80995

Hearts at Home
900 W. College Ave.
Normal, IL 61761

Masterful Living
Pam and Bill Farrel
629 S. Rancho Santa Fe #306
San Marcos, CA 92069

Moms in Touch
PO Box 35500
Colorado Springs, CO 80935

MOPS (Mothers of Preschoolers)
PO Box 102200
Denver, CO 80250-2200

Parent Talk
PO Box 3700
Tucson, AZ 85740

NOTES

Chapter 3

1. Brenda Hunter, *Where Have All the Mothers Gone?* (Grand Rapids, MI: Zondervan, 1982), pp. 92-93.

2. Ibid., p. 90.

Chapter 4

1. You may contact: Mom's Jar of Preserves Company, 991 C Lomas Santa Fe #435, Solana Beach, CA, 92075.

2. Many thanks to Pam, Esther, Kristi, Tammy, Michele, Maria, Kristina, Tracey, and Jay—all wonderfully creative moms!

Chapter 6

1. Sheila Brownlow, Rebecca Whitener, and Janet M. Rupert, "'I'll Take Gender Differences for $1000!' Domain-Specific Intellectual: Success on *Jeopardy*," *Sex Roles* (New York, Feb. 1998). Obtained via ProQuest, a Bell & Howell information service.

2. Ibid.

3. Florence Littauer, *Raising Christians—Not Just Children* (Dallas, TX: Word, 1988), p. 73.

4. Ibid., p. 54.

5. Kevin Leman, *The New Birth Order Book: Why You Are the Way You Are* (Grand Rapids, MI: Revell, 1988), p. 15.

6. Ibid., p. 16.

7. Ibid., p. 18.

8. Ibid., p. 187.

9. Cynthia Tobias, *The Way They Learn* (Colorado Springs, CO: Focus on the Family, 1994), p. 19.

10. Ibid., adapted from pages 91-96.

11. Gary Chapman, *The Five Love Languages of Teenagers* (Chicago, IL: Northfield Publishing, 2000), p. 127.

12. Ibid., p. 128.

13. For "Caught You Being Good" stickers, contact More Hours in My Day by calling Sheri Torelli at 909/682-4714.

Chapter 7

1. Stormie Omartian, *The Power of a Praying™ Parent* (Eugene, OR: Harvest House, 1995), p. 14.

Chapter 8

1. Cheri Fuller and Louise Tucker Jones, *Extraordinary Kids* (Colorado Springs, CO: Focus on the Family, 1997), pp. 26-28.

2. Ibid., pp. 33-34.

3. Ibid., p. 38.

4. H. Norman Wright, *Loving a Prodigal* (Colorado Springs, CO: Chariot Victor, 1999), p. 53-54.

5. Ibid., p. 50.

6. Gleason Archer, *Encyclopedia of Biblical Difficulties* (Grand Rapids, MI: Zondervan, 1982), p. 253.

Chapter 10

1. Os Guinness, *The Call* (Nashville, TN: Word, 1998), p. 46.

2. Carol Kuykendall, *Give Them Wings* (Wheaton, IL: Tyndale, 1994), p. 60.

3. Ibid., p. 62.

4. Ibid., p. 157.

For more resources to enhance your parenting or to connect with Pam and Bill Farrel for a speaking engagement, contact:

Masterful Living
629 S Rancho Santa Fe #306
San Marcos, CA 92069
(760) 727-9122

www.Masterfulliving.com
Email: mliving@webcc.net

Other Good
Harvest House Reading

Men Are like Waffles—Women Are like Spaghetti
Bill and Pam Farrel

The Farrels explain why a man is like a waffle (each element of his life is in a separate box), why a woman is like spaghetti (everything in her life touches everything else), and what these differences mean. Then they show you how to achieve more satisfying relationships. Biblical insights, sound research, humorous anecdotes, and real-life stories make this book entertaining and practical.

A Woman God Can Use
Pam Farrel

Sharing stories and insights on God's desires for us, Pam helps you sense His approval. You will discover how to please God, focus creativity and enthusiasm, and live life based on biblical truth.

The Power of a Praying™ Parent
Stormie Omartian

Popular author and singer Stormie Omartian offers 30 easy-to-read chapters that focus on specific areas of prayers for parents. This personal, practical guide leads the way to enriched, strong prayer lives for parents.

Taking Flight from the Empty Nest
Mary Jenson

When the last child leaves home, many women feel lonely, depressed, and unsure about themselves and their future. It doesn't have to be that way! Acclaimed author Mary Jenson shares her journey to viewing this transition as an exciting beginning. Combining unflinching honesty with humor, *Taking Flight from the Empty Nest* will inspire and challenge every mother who "isn't ready to let go" or wonders "what's next?"

The Things That Matter Most
Bob Welch

In this new collection of warm and personal stories, Gold Medallion award winning author Bob Welch directs you back to the things that matter most:

family love, deep-down character, time spent with each other, and memories rooted in things that are true and lasting. As you encounter meaning and truth drawn from the everyday events that shape your life, Bob's stories will make you laugh, make you cry, but above all will make you stop and think—about relationships, about the people around you whom you love, about moving away from the materialism that tugs at our hearts and minds every day.

A Father for All Seasons
Bob Welch

This highly personal book gives encouragement to fathers and sons by reminding them that they need each other. Excerpts of this book have appeared in *Focus on the Family* and *Reader's Digest* magazines.

Where Roots Grow Deep
Bob Welch

Bob Welch offers powerfully touching true stories written with humor and rich insight that highlight the joy of creating a legacy of love for your family and the generations to come.